...keeping Clarke.

One son. One day.
One mom's personal
journey through grief.

Stephanie Benbenek

To all who grieve

Acknowledgments

During the bleak times following Clarke's death, anything that came into my mind ended up on paper—any kind of paper: napkins, used envelopes, church bulletins, pages in a sudoku book. Ideas, thoughts, phrases, stories, scraps of memories, even dreams, and coincidences that defied normal explanation.

After almost two years, I began to believe that my grieving experience was worth sharing with others. While I agree that writing can be therapeutic and cathartic, this was something more—much more. Many times I felt the words coming *through me* rather than *out of me*. These scribblings became "Clarke's book." Many times I felt a divine inspiration and a whisper in my ear, "Mom, you gotta finish this." Many times, blinded by tears, I wrote by feel.

So here it is—my heart, my soul, my darkest corner, and my brightest star. ... *keeping Clarke.* is what I have, and I give it to you. But I couldn't have done it alone.

Thank you to Nance Piggins—editor extraordinaire—for knowing exactly what Clarke wanted me to say. You lovingly read each word in ... *keeping Clarke.* a hundred times and helped me form them into this book. My gypsy sister!

Thank you to Holly, my best friend of thirty-five years, who spent years and countless hours listening to me, crying with me, supporting me, and continuing to love me as I took my first painful steps toward a life without Clarke. Especially thank you for "the pause button."

To all of Clarke's family—grandparents, uncles, aunts, cousins—I know that there's a hole in your heart, too. My hope is that you can be filled with the love and memory of Clarke.

Thank you to so many caring, supportive, prayerful, and loving friends and family who made … *keeping Clarke.* possible. At the risk of leaving someone out, let me simply say, you know who you are; I certainly do. I will never forget what you have done and continue to do. I hope that you are aware of my love for you and your families.

Thank you to all of Clarke's friends—especially the Mauldin 7 and Charlie Company 2008, Forever Casual—you feel his absence, but you are keeping Clarke through memories of him and your time together.

Thank you to my pastors—the "Revrunds" Dr. David Taylor and Tandy Taylor. Your faithfulness pulled me through my "night season" and has inspired me to be a better person. "Whoo!"

To Elizabeth Baker of Long Island, New York; a fearless mother who held Clarke's hand and prayed over him as his spirit left his body.

To Ashley for the brother she never knew.

...keeping Clarke.

And most importantly, to my husband, Scott. "I FINISHED IT!"

We met at age fourteen, fell in love in our twenties, and much later, married in our forties. I know this isn't the journey we expected, but I can't imagine going through this without you. Everyday, I thank God that we're together. I love you.

Chapter 1

It was one of those early February Fridays in Charleston, South Carolina, when the morning would dawn and the fog chill would hover above the grass like a sheer voile hanky. By midafternoon, with the sun deceivingly bright, you could position yourself in a direct beam and feel the promise of spring in its warmth, although your toes could still feel the tingle of frostbite.

I had come to the coast with some well-meaning girl friends who had encouraged me to join them, hoping the trip would lift my spirits. One of the gals owns a condo in Wild Dunes on the Isle of Palms, one of my very favorite Charleston places and only three and a half hours from where my husband and I lived in Simpsonville, in the Upstate of South Carolina.

I've always loved it here—travelling between Charleston and Myrtle Beach most of my life—girls' trips, family trips, and anytime-I-just-needed-to-get-away trips. Somethin' about rollin' down your window once you get close to the South Carolina coast, inhaling deeply, and smelling oysters perched on top of dimpled mud hills during low tide. Palms and palmettos simultaneously waving in tune with bursts of the winds, "Hello, Stephanie ... so glad you're back." And of course the nucleus of it all—the majestic Atlantic Ocean that stretches forever to the other side of the world. Never changing—tides in, tides out, tides in. For me, the ocean has always affirmed my belief in God, although I honestly can't tell you why, specifically. Maybe it's because I feel small and insignificant in the scheme of the ocean's vast, cyclical power.

This particular Friday, I was certain that I had grown even smaller still, to the point that perhaps I may just disappear. Or maybe the ocean really wasn't as awesome as I had thought it was for so many years. Although for sure, one thing was quite clear to me: Charleston just wasn't working its magic for me like it used to. Could anything change my spirits? If not the ocean or the palms or the oystered aromas, then what?

Later that morning after we had arrived, some of the girls suggested we all do a little island shopping. For some inexplicable reason that never really started out as a logical, rational thought, I decided instead that I would pay a visit to the Citadel Military College and catch the Friday parade. Every Friday afternoon, rain or shine, the same procession of the Corps of Cadets performed in the same way, as it has for over 163 years. Never to change—this stunning full-dress tradition. You could boil your eggs by its precision, just like the tides. *When things seem to be falling apart, there's nothing like simple tradition to keep the loose threads from totally unraveling.* You could count on the parade at the Citadel happening every Friday, rain or shine.

I didn't have to survey the parade field: I knew it well from memory. How many times had I stood right over there, where First Battalion exits the barracks to enter the parade? Then, moving ever so slowly to the front of the crowd (so as not to seem rude), I would bob here and there to get the best damn look possible at Charlie Company. Row 2. Outside right. Rifle on shoulder. Taller than most—Clarke, my son. His long legs in starched white pants—left up, left down, right up, right down, every movement and muscle in regimented cadence. His eyes, straight ahead, not daring to break the strict discipline of "cuttin' Momma a glance." And I, knowing full well that afterward when we had time together, Clarke would say, "Mom, didja' see that pigeon at parade today?" I'd always reply, "What pigeon, hon?" And Clarke would smirk, "I don't know … there was just some funky pigeon … looked like you, bobbing its head up and down, to get a better look." So I resembled a pigeon? The nerve! I embraced every loving jab.

Unlike every other time I had attended Friday parade, today I opted to view the event from the far right corner of the field. As it happened, there was a strong, sturdy Pin Oak tree standing exactly in my chosen spot—its branches, in need of a trim, spilling out and down, creating a waterfall of miniature leaves that gave me a shield for emotional privacy. I ducked under the leafy canopy right away, nearly twisting my ankle on the humungous, thick, and partially emerged roots that slithered out like petrified pythons to a ground radius of about five feet around the tree's base. And so, I was here. Alone. Under the camouflage of drooping oak branches. And definitely not part of the growing, happy crowd lining the sidewalks behind the field stanchions. I pushed my way through the green curtain to the very front hanging branch. The glint of digital cameras flashing from extremely proud parents gave the spectator area in front of me the appearance of one long, progressive sparkler.

My sense of seclusion and safety was suddenly broken by three deep reverberations of bells from Summerall Chapel. Friday Parade had begun. I heard the bagpipes follow immediately in the distance, becoming more forceful and plaintive the closer they approached. This leading band formed a large rectangle of Citadel "Highlanders" in movement, tasseled boots and kilt pleats of blue tartan plaid kicking out from their muscled knees. At the head of this rectangle was a gigantic upperclassman cadet in military uniform and in his hand, a large, crude, scepterlike wooden baton. Behind him, one lone cadet drummer was strapped with a drum that was as big around as he was tall. Around his shoulders hung a stole of ferocious leopard fur, like a victorious warrior coming back from battle. Following him were four rows, consisting of the bagpipe, horn, cymbal, drum, and tuba sections. All of the musicians were clad in the dress of the clan. Friday parade at the Citadel—a weekly event that, no matter how many times you watched, it always felt like it was the first.

Clarke loved tradition. This was one of his most favorite things of all about attending the Citadel. I thought about him and his experiences here. How like a Petri dish this college is— growing scared eighteen-year-olds on an agar of discipline, physical and mental toughness, honor, and brotherhood. I couldn't believe how quickly Clarke had matured and thrived in this environment. Everyone had joked and said he had *really* gone from Clarke to Superman in a little over a year, always dubbed Superman, of course because of his name.

Although I was overcome by emotion, I somehow found the strength to step out from my protective lair—now I was in full view of the approaching companies. Delta, then Charlie— Clarke's company, followed by Bravo and Alpha—all in First Battalion. Every one of the cadets from Charlie Company saw me standing there and then did something absolutely out of the normal discipline. Something that I believe shocked even them. In unison, the cadets turned their heads to the left and nodded solemnly to me in a show of respect. Several cadets in the other three companies did the same.

At once, I felt an incredible, internal void. I remember asking myself, *Is this what it will feel like for the rest of my life; this aching intensity of a longing for events that will never happen again? Of surrendering hopes and dreams for an unfinished life?* And I realized—at that very moment—this void would, in varying degrees, be with me forever. I knew that I would have to live a different life now. Without the Citadel. Without Friday Parade. Without Clarke. It had been nearly four months since he was killed.

I Believe …

I believe that everyone wishes to be kept.

It's why we write our names with a driftwood stylus in the wet sands of beaches, why we carve initials in the bark of hard oaks and soft pines, why the first survivors coaled stick figures on ragged rock.

If only for a brief time—before the ocean's waves fill the grooves and wash away our autograph, before the tree is hewn for another purpose, before the moss grows over the ancient art—we seek our indelible mark…yearning to be kept and remembered.

As I was growing up, I recall many reminders to keep the faith, keep my chin up, keep a secret, keep in touch, keep a promise. *(Now I lay me down to sleep, I pray the Lord my soul to keep.)*

So why is it that when we experience death's vacuous, hopeless hollow, does keeping stop? Instead of keeping we are encouraged to let go. "You'll get over it. Time will heal and help you forget. The sooner you let go, the sooner you can move on with your life." Instead of preparing us to abandon, why doesn't society teach us the peace of mind that comes with keeping? After all, keeping is simply managing pain in search of a different outcome and a different outlook. A *"keeping state of mind"* is a way for those who grieve to move forward and live with honor, respect, love. And hope.

I keep Clarke by living. I live by keeping Clarke.

Chapter 2

When one hears that his or her child has been killed, there is an inclination to either become paralyzed, run away from, or oppose the grief. But what shock does for a human being is truly remarkable. It is the armor that keeps us moving, existing, functioning, until we are just one millionth of a percent ready to face life. As shock wanes, real grief sets in.

Psychologists tell us that the human responses to any difficult situation fall within three categories: fight, flight, or freeze. Unless, of course, your child dies. Then it's an entirely different difficult situation for which I believe there is an additional fourth response: fight, flight, freeze, or *embrace*. Only by embracing or succumbing to the process of grief was I truly able to push into a new life.

From this day on and each day hereafter, I will choose to embrace you, grief. Because I expect that you will bring me down in six days, six months, six years, or beyond. I want you to attack me now, while you're in your larval stage (*before you have real teeth*). Come on, I urge, you who has suffocated me in my waking moments, my doing moments, my sleeping moments. I do not want you hibernating inside of me, and then waking up after you have rested plenty, ravenous and eager to take me down. I want you before you invade every cell of my body. I want your cancer in its early stages, not insidiously multiplying inside of me to find me powerless one day, unable to take my life back. Yes, I succumb to you, grief. In fact, I believe I'm actually dancing with you. You and I will always be in a constant struggle to take the lead.

So it is that almost immediately, I decided to write about my experience. One, to embrace my grief. And two, because of the surprisingly few resources to connect with, when one's child dies, specifically losing that child to a sudden, tragic, and shocking circumstance. My wound is vast and bisects my body. Since the shock has begun to fall away piece by piece, the reality is that I have good days and then bad days. Strange how every really bad day makes for a better day the next. It's as though my tears act as an antiseptic to keep my mortal wound from becoming infected, from breeding gangrene, from destroying my whole being from the inside out. This I can't allow; who I am, to a great degree, is who my son was. Many times, usually after I have been suffering for a prolonged period, I believe I hear my Clarke insisting, "All right, that's enough, Mom. You've got places to go and people to see. GET UP." I know that he is right. It would be so very simple to numb myself with a few anti-anxiety pills, get in my bed, slip away beneath the covers and disappear into dreams of before. Speech and sight and feelings, forever muffled by cotton blankets. How easy that would be. But my son never did the easy thing. In our likeness and in his honor, neither will I.

When Clarke could have attended a college where both the fraternities *and* the fraternizing were aplenty, he instead chose the Citadel—the Military College of South Carolina. *(Don't ask—we still can't figure out why!)* His rigorous freshman year was an experience in growth, maturity, and great discipline. Up at 6:00 a.m., mandatory study, curfew *always*, grueling physical requirements, a total breakdown of who he thought he was, rebuilt to be the man he was to become. I was impressed, Clarke's father was impressed, and my husband, Scott—Clarke's stepfather—was totally blown away, to the point where he had to eat his own words. The meal consisted of, "We'll be back to pick him up in two weeks. I mean, come on ... Clarke can't even set his own alarm clock for high school!" Lunch anyone? Clarke fooled us all. He not only attended the Citadel, he attended well, acing his freshman, "Knob" year and making Dean's List both semesters.

Chapter 3

Clarke had been looking forward to going to the Citadel-Florida State University football game. Overnight arrangements, the food, the munchies are all readied for him and his friends—the three of them, due to arrive in Tallahassee Saturday, September 10, to cheer on their Citadel Bulldogs, with time to spare for enough meaningful tailgating.

We actually heard about these travel plans from Clarke himself, the weekend just before that Citadel-Florida State University game. Flashback: Labor Day weekend and lucky for us, Clarke is coming home. I say "lucky" because, unlike most other cadets, Clarke is given a pass to come home for Labor Day—a weekend during which the Citadel campus in Charleston is, for all intents and purposes, "closed." Few cadets are allowed to leave, but because my baby has achieved the Dean's List twice during freshman year, he is awarded his first weekend leave pass as a sophomore, and Clarke chooses Labor Day weekend. Lucky. He catches a ride home to Simpsonville, SC, early on Saturday morning, September 3. Of course, his weekend plans are already well in the works, including a trip to a Clemson football game with all of his buddies who attend the university there. Knowing well in advance his intentions for this Saturday night, I have gone ahead and treated Clarke and his Clemson friends to tickets on the fifty-yard line and even a parking pass right outside the stadium. Mix in the postgame SAE fraternity party with his "hometown posse," and man do they end up having *one* great time.

As he leaves for the Clemson game, Clarke says to us, "I'll be home early tomorrow morning to have some family time."

Scott laughs when I share Clarke's statement, "I've never heard him say that before. What's up with that?"

Clarke has brought home a bulging bag of laundry; along with a strict verbal warning that one particular clump of his dirty clothes will be absolutely, no doubt, offensive. He had worn them the previous Thursday during rugby practice. He laughs and says that maybe I'll want to put on a filter mask, just in case. He's right. The clothes are still wet with his sweat, a day and a half in a hot laundry bag. Whew!

Within the hour of his Labor Day weekend arrival home, I fix us both a sandwich as we talk and joke about his challenging classes this semester—he's taking twenty hours and shooting for the Dean's List a third time. Between his ravenous chomps and great gulps of milk, I listen intently—amused as he describes funny incidents about himself and his cadet buddies. He is laughing so hard at one point his milk starts to come out of his nostrils. After yet another one of these lunches with my son that never ever seems long enough, I go into the laundry room to tackle the mountain of stinky wash. As Clarke heads upstairs to crash for a while and rest up for the night ahead with his friends, he asks, "Mom, will you wake me up at one thirty? No later?" I promise. He bounds up the stairs three at a time, climbs into bed, and falls asleep almost at once. Clarke never ever has a problem sleeping, especially in his own bed.

As promised, at one thirty, I arrive upstairs, stopping short of waking him, standing next to his bed, watching him sleep for as long as four minutes, maybe more. I am quiet—a mother mouse. At nineteen, three months shy of twenty, Clarke is a beautiful young man, inside and out. My only child—his dad and I did right well by this one! As I watch his steady breath, I am overwhelmed with my own profound pride in him. Or is

14

it appreciation, a gratitude that goes beyond feeling lucky he is home for a weekend to feeling lucky that this boy is my son? I look above his headboard and see the three crosses we hung there last year. "Father, Son, and Holy Ghost," we had said. Triple protection. Fighting to shake this near trance I've entered, I see the clock has changed from one thirty to one thirty-five. Strangely, somehow, this moment seems important for me. I don't know why I stand over Clarke today. I haven't done this since he was a toddler. I gently shake his shoulder to wake him.

Chapter 4

On Sunday, the next morning, I'll be damned if he doesn't come home early from Clemson—just like he said he would. We are together nearly the entire Sunday, and again I become consumed with the easy way in which Clarke details his time the night before with his special friends. Later on, we chill and watch some of the movie *Goodfellas*. Could be watchin' paint dry for all I care—my son Clarke is home. Once again, my house and my heart are full. I grill a beef filet so he has a good old-fashioned "Mom's dinner" before returning to mess hall grub. When I call him to the table, he grabs the plate, closes his eyes as he waves it under his nose, then takes a long inhale, and says, "Mom, you treat me like a king." I shoot back, "Honey," cocking my head toward the den where his stepfather is reading the Sunday paper, "that there's the king … he brings home the bacon, but you sure are the prince!" Hearing this exchange, Scott looks in the kitchen, folds his paper, and wanders in to join us at the table.

Between bites (*Honey, puhleez eat with your mouth closed!*), and in anticipation of his upcoming travels the very next weekend, Clarke asks Scott, "Really, how cool is it when that Indian rides his horse out on the field before the game?" He is, of course, referring to the Florida State mascot, Seminole Chief Osceola, in full and fierce feather headdress. As tradition has it, at the start of each game, Chief Osceola rides out to the middle of the field on a magnificent horse, with flaming spear in hand. The fans go wild, and as the screams get louder, the chief commandeers his steed into several circles, and then in a dramatic gesture, stabs the fifty-yard line with the fiery spear and gives a blood-chilling Indian cry. The fans go even crazier. This is war. "Seriously, how cool is it?" Clarke begs his stepdad. "Way cool, son. Way cool."

Two years after Clarke was killed, I looked at Scott one evening and erupted with tears. Kicking myself in the heart and wringing my hands, I implored, "Why did we have to encourage him with that mascot shit?" Scott could not answer. He just looked at me and shook his head sadly. I rushed, "Why did we say that? Maybe if we wouldn't have said it … maybe he wouldn't have been so high on going to the game." But my words could not change what had happened. To this day, I could painfully search for each infinitesimal scenario, word, comment or action that may have altered the course of events of September 10, 2005. But were I to find them now, what could I possibly do with them? They are ashes, as fine as powder, slipping through my hands. It is too late. I must put these thoughts away. They can, I know, destroy me.

When Clarke's car pool ride back to Charleston arrives late that Sunday afternoon, Clarke grabs his laundry bag— now filled with perfectly clean and folded clothes—plus a container of chocolate chip bars that I baked between wash loads. He kisses me briskly and says "Love you, Mom." Just like that, he is out the door headed back to the Citadel.

Chapter 5

I talk to my son several times that next week after our Labor Day visit. Our conversations are short and sweet. He has a lot going on and way too many instant messages to juggle to be talking to his mom all the time. Clarke and I never end a phone conversation without saying "I love you." I speak with him Friday, September 9, before dress parade. He tells me that some close friends from high school are driving in to have dinner with him that night. I can't hold back the slight suggestion that maybe *after* dress parade and *before* his buds get there he might be able to study for a huge Spanish test he has coming up on Monday. We have a good chuckle on that. Like he has studying on his mind—with best pals and dinner plans that night *and* the big Florida State game he plans to attend with his other Citadel buds the next morning. Ha. No kid can be a prince all the time, no matter what a Southern momma thinks.

I have his receipt for $11.45, dated 9/10 at 9:10 a.m. Heading for the football game on Saturday morning, Clarke and his two Citadel classmates, Brett and Blake (who also call Simpsonville home), pull into Bojangles to wolf down some breakfast and change from their stiff school uniforms into more casual "civvies"—the kind of civvies only a mom could wash, dry, and fold so meticulously the weekend before. Clarke buys the biscuits. They eat, then get back on the road, and never make it out of Charleston. The vehicle they're driving merges onto I-95 at mile marker 82. Within a mile of the entrance ramp, the right rear tire comes apart, and the car is airborne, bursting into a haze of dust and metal. It flips violently several times. *Did you know that with each flip, the chances of any occupant surviving a rollover decreases by 25 percent? I know this now. I also know that the right rear tire is the worst tire to lose. Loss of that particular tire position makes a vehicle the most unstable.*

The driver, Brett, and the backseat passenger, Blake, are both thrown from the metallic gold, late model, Mitsubishi Montero Sport. When the car comes to rest in the median, Clarke is the only person in it. (I imagine that he called shotgun that morning as I had heard him and his friends claim so many times before.) Clarke has his seat belt securely fastened. His seat is as far back as it can go. Even after the turbulent rolling and landing, Clarke's civvies remain unruffled, from the familiar baseball cap and the Costa del Mar shades down to the Rainbow flip-flops. Everything on his exterior body is intact. All three boys—all nineteen years old—all from Simpsonville, South Carolina. The two front-seat occupants, Clarke and Brett, die at the scene—as later explained to me by both the Dorchester County Coroner and the highway patrol supervisor. Blake lives six more days.

Clarke's time of death: 9:50 a.m. Saturday, September 10, 2005. My only child, my life, my angel—a young man with so much promise that I weep daily for his missed opportunities. The entire story and circumstances of how I came to know that my son died that day are bizarre; the accident scenario seems frequently unbelievable and surreal, as though Clarke is still at school, or maybe this really *is* a horrible nightmare from which I cannot awaken. Of all the people that I know and have known in my lifetime, I never thought this would happen to me, to my son. But it did, and God knows I am trying to hold on.

Chapter 6

Friday, September 9

I have an invigorating run on the treadmill and finish at 8:30 a.m. Clarke calls around 3:00 p.m., excitedly reminding me of his Friday night dinner plans in Charleston, and of course—that he and his Citadel classmates are leaving for the Florida State game in Tallahassee the next morning. He is definitely "jacked"—even about the six-hour drive down.

I speak with Clarke again briefly at 5:58 p.m. that same day. He wants me to know that he and his buds have a place to stay in Tallahassee on Saturday night, and not to worry.

"Mom, we've got everything thought out. And we won't be drinkin' and drivin'."

"I'm glad honey. I know y'all plan to tailgate—I'm just lettin' you know you better be smart enough to 'park it.'" I tell him to have a fantastic weekend (God knows these Citadel cadets deserve it), but not to forget his big Spanish test on Monday.

"I won't forget," he assures me. Then before we hang up, we tell each other "I love you."

I end as always, "Be careful." Four minutes later, I succumb to an incredible feeling—that "I need to know *just … one … more … thing*" feeling and call Clarke again. This time, *enough already, Mom!* This time, I get voice mail, but leave this very cryptic message from a caring mom. "You guys switch off driving tomorrow … help each other out." Then, as an involuntary comment, I add, "I really wish you weren't going to FSU, but I'm sure that's just wishing on the wind." I can see him rolling his eyes at this message.

The rest of the night I'm in a funk—a bonafide foul, swampy mood. There is no making me feel better. I am definitely in bitch mode. I don't know why, but it is a feeling that is not my usual "Stephanie self." Worse yet, it's a feeling that I can't seem to shake. This heavy angst decides to follow me into Saturday morning and plant itself squarely on my shoulders.

Chapter 7

Saturday, September 10

Scott has a golf match today. Before he leaves the house at 8:30 a.m., we have words; no, not words—that sounds too civilized. Actually, I scream at him. Half serious and half joking, he asks, "What is the matter with you? Are you on some kind of new medication, or do you *need* medication?" Exasperated, I say, "Exactly what the hell are you talking about?" Being a bright man and knowing that no good can possibly come from this conversation, he leaves early for his golf game. When I am in this state of mind, I can be quick on the trigger, make absolutely no sense, and allow my mean side to show a most unpleasant face. How smart of him to find a way out of what is shaping up to be a really combative exchange. Hoping to do the same, I turn to exercise—my proven remedy for releasing frustration that's as close and convenient as my first floor office. I step on the rubber belt, hit start, and go hard for thirty-five minutes, hands pumping and feet stomping.

I grab a towel, start to wipe the sweat off my face and neck, and walk through my bedroom to the shower. The phone rings.

"Hello, Steph, how are ya'?" It's my brother, Tony. Without bothering to hear how I really am, he cuts off my response with, "Hey, what's Clarke's mobile number?"

"Have you lost it again?" I ask, exasperated. *I'm already in a bad enough mood without adding an extra measure of annoyed.*

"Yeah, you know it's tough for me to keep up with everybody's numbers, but I asked Clarke to get me a Florida State hat while he's down in Tallahassee. Just want to remind him."

"Don't worry," I try to say as politely as I can—in my current frame of mind, dealing with an annoying brother is like playing with a loaded weapon—somebody's going to go off. "I'll call him for you. I want to see where they are on the road anyway."

"Okay, tell him not to forget."

My day continues to move forward, and yet I still feel stuck in first gear. My feet seem to be weighted. Two concrete blocks attached to my ankles. Today, everything's bugging me. I hang up with my brother and dial Clarke's number at 9:06 a.m. Voice mail kicks in. "Hey, hon, Uncle Tony just called to remind you about picking him up an FSU hat. Call me. Love you. Bye." There are some errands I can run, and ultimately weighing the inactivity versus the activity, decide to do exactly that in hopes of shaking loose this funky blanket on an otherwise sunny South Carolina Saturday. Then, I continue to encourage myself. When I get back home, there's plenty of yard work I can do—no, actually must do. Besides, I really don't have time to sit about feelin' bad for myself. My sister and her husband are coming to grill steaks with us tonight. We'll watch the South Carolina-Georgia football game; have a few cocktails, and a perfectly cooked dinner. Scott and I were actually supposed to attend that game in Georgia, but I had said, "No, I really don't feel like going to Athens today." Today I'm just not into it. Any of it.

By midday, after the have-to errands, I'm back at home and dressed in my "yard" shorts, tank top, and a lovely skin tone I'll call sweaty dirt-brown—from head to toe. I speak with a friend of mine, Susan, whose son, Logan, also attends the Citadel. Another good friend of Clarke's (he was always blessed to have so many good friends), Logan is confined to barracks that day for a merit infraction. At the Citadel, infractions equal walking tours, which are measured in miles. The more infractions, the more miles you have to walk off. Susan and I chat, laugh, and wonder out loud, "Will he ever be finished with his tours?" We also talk about the current weather topic, Hurricane Ophelia, which at that very moment is skirting the coast of South Carolina and causing all of us who have children attending college in Charleston to tune to the Weather Channel.

I return to digging in the dirt in hopes of cultivating—what? Maybe, I guess, just a better mood. My cell rings. It's Susan again. "Way-ull," she announces in her heavy Southern drawl, "have you heard? They're evacuating the Citadel for Ophelia." We both break out in a roar of laughter. I say, "I'll bet Clarke and his friends get down to Tallahassee for the football game, only to have to turn right around and head back to the Citadel! Let me go call him, and I'll call you right back." I dial Clarke's number at 4:04 p.m. and get his voice mail again. "Honey," I start, "I don't know if you've heard, but the Citadel's being evacuated, so y'all just might have to drive directly back to Charleston, get your school stuff together, and come home. If any of your buds need a place to stay, bring 'em on! Bye ... love you ... call me." I call Susan again and tell her, "I'm having no luck reaching Clarke. I just keep getting his voice mail." She says she'll make a couple of calls, nail down some mobile numbers if possible, and call me back.

When I haven't heard back from Susan after about thirty minutes, I dial her home number and her husband, Tim, answers. Quickly and way, way too abruptly, Tim tells me Susan is on her way to my house and should be here in a few minutes. "Uh, okay," I say. The way the conversation ends and Tim's general demeanor don't sit well with me. I'm in the garage, phone still in hand, with a quizzical look on my face when Scott pulls into the driveway from his golf game. "I just had a strange thing happen," I tell him. I relay the information about Tim telling me that Susan is coming over. "Now, why's she comin' over here? I've been talking to her off and on all day. She never even mentioned maybe coming over. She never even mentioned stopping by. She never even called to say she was on her way."

I then try to call Susan's home number again. No answer. Her mobile. No answer. Home, again. Voice mail. Mobile, again. Voice mail. "Susan, why aren't you answering your mobile? Tim says you're headed over. Now he won't answer the home phone, and you won't answer your cell. What's goin' on?" Scott is in the bedroom undressing, and I hear the shower start. I am pacing. I am muttering. My thoughts are ricocheting back and forth. *Something's goin' on. Why can't I get anyone to answer the phone?* Scott calls out into the great room, "What's up, Steph? You're antsy as hell." I answer, "Don't know, but it's somethin'."

I finally get an idea to call Susan's son myself at the Citadel. After all he is confined to barracks—at least I know where he is. I'm not the kind to wait, and this day—this moment that is lasting a lifetime—is no exception. "Hey, Logan." "Hey, Miss Stephanie." *You can be eighty years old, married for fifty, but in the South you are always "Miss" somebody.* I continue, "I'm trying to get your dad or your mom, but no one will pick up the phone." "Did you try my dad's mobile?" Logan asks hesitantly. "No, I don't have that number. Give it to me." I jot it down. "Okay, thanks, dear." As quickly as I hang up with Logan, my mobile rings for the second or third time. I don't remember. Caller ID identifies two of my girlfriends have called. They're probably calling to get together for a glass of wine later this afternoon. They are great fun, but I'm too focused on dialing and redialing Susan's home and mobile numbers to answer personal calls. Not now.

Chapter 8

I'm standing just outside my garage in the grass at the end of my driveway, and I dial the number Logan has given me to reach his dad. His dad automatically answers his cell. I say, "Tim, it's Steph again. Why's Susan on her way to my house? What's this all about?" After a sound that resembles paper ripping, I hear Tim begin to cry. When I hear this man trying to talk through his tears, I drop to my knees on the grass. I'm faintly aware of a power lifting my spirit out of my body. Tim sobs, "Susan will be there in a minute." Somewhere in my brain the question screams, *"Why is this man crying?" Why is this man crying?"* My mind struggles to register a connection.

An indescribable feeling comes over my whole being. Instinct automatically takes over. Blood and veins converge to burst. I know that if this man, if any man, is sobbing in the phone to me that he knows something. Something that I don't know. Something that is horribly wrong on his end. The bad news is that I am on the other end. Uncontrollably, I begin to sob, I scream, and then plead, "Tim!" He continues to cry. I am weak, and I feel all the air knocked out of my body. He says between breaths, "All I know, Stephanie, is that there's been an accident." I feel like I am slipping into a glass jar and the glass is closing around me. I cannot get up from the ground. I clutch the phone, and I am screaming at Tim, *the all knowing one on the other end,* "YOU SWEAR TO GOD THAT YOU DON'T KNOW ANYTHING ELSE? YOU SWEAR TO GOD? YOU SWEAR TO GOD ON YOUR CHILDREN, TIM? PLEASE. TELL ME. PLEASE. WHAT DO YOU KNOW?" I am begging him with tears running down my dirty face and then I fully collapse into the blades of grass. He cries, "Susan will be there. Just wait for her, please ..." and then the connection is lost. He knows if he stays on the phone a moment longer he will have no choice but to blurt out the truth.

I get up, run through the garage, and stumble in my back door. I fall onto the kitchen floor, and with a Geronimo scream, I yell out to Scott, "*THERE'S BEEN AN ACCIDENT!*" Scott tries to hear me over his shower and yells, "*HONEY, WHAT DID YOU SAY?*" I scream, louder this time, "*THERE'S... BEEN... AN... ACCIDENT!*" I hear a silence and then his two words, "Oh Lord." Now he is in the kitchen with a towel wrapped around his waist. I'm out of my mind with fear and hysteria—not knowing what it is I'm supposed to know. I'm lying on the large sand colored rug in front of the refrigerator. I get up, look frantically at Scott, and he says, "What happened?" I howl, "I *DON'T KNOW.* Tim said he didn't know anything and that Susan will be here *AND TIM WAS CRY... UH... UH... UH... ING...* Oh my God, what is happening?" Scott is frozen.

There's a knock at the back door. I run to it, jerk the door open, and see Susan standing there. Her eyes are fixed on me, and they are shockingly bright, and the entire lower half of her face is trembling. A man is standing behind her who is dressed in black and white, and my first thought is, "Why is Susan's pastor here with her?" She throws her arms around me and keeps saying, "We are here for you," and I keep screaming, "*WHAT HAS HAPPENED? FOR GOD'S SAKE, TELL ME WHAT'S HAPPENED! YOU ARE HERE FOR ME FOR WHAT?*" Then on my right side periphery, I see that the man previously standing behind Susan is now sitting at my kitchen table. Scott, who miraculously has changed from his bath towel into a pair of shorts and a shirt, is standing behind me and facing the stranger. At that moment I realize Susan hasn't a clue who the man is, either. He is not with her but has merely arrived at my house at exactly the same time.

I hear the stranger's words, soft and methodical— something about the vehicle and a tire malfunction on I-95 and something about Clarke Russell, my Clarke, dying at the scene. My voice is far away. *"NOOOOOO!"*

I am breathing as deeply as a human can—gulping air to find power against the finality of words that have been spoken. On the exhale, *am I screaming? "NOT MY CLARKE, NOT MY CHILD, THIS (gasp) IS (gasp) NOT (gasp) HAPPENINNNG!"* Scott comes up to me from behind and wraps his arms around me, pinning my arms to my body. I bend at the waist, thankful that he is there. He lifts me slightly off my feet to keep me standing. I reach out for my kitchen island. Its ceramic surface is hard and cold. It is something that I can hold onto. I am trying to slap my senses to attention from this scene, this unspeakable, unthinkable drama that is acting out in front of me. "Who are you?" I hear Scott ask of the man sitting at my kitchen table on this beautiful afternoon. "I am the Greenville County Coroner," he says. The time is 4:50 p.m. Clarke died this morning at 9:50 a.m.

Chapter 9

I often say that if you need to get the word out or evacuate an entire city, tell one teenager with a cell phone. This tragic event was no exception. Word spread quickly. Friends from the University of South Carolina, Citadel, Clemson, and the College of Charleston are getting the news that something horrible has happened. They call each other at football games, at home, and in their cars. With the first phone call (I'm not quite sure who initiated the chain), it spreads like a computer virus. Someone hears and calls someone else. All of Clarke's friends from middle school to high school to college know by 2:00 p.m. that he is dead. He dies in this accident before I leave my house to do my errands earlier this morning. He dies right after I leave the voicemail about the FSU hat for his uncle Tony. At the moment of his death, 9:50 a.m., I was probably finishing my third and final cup of coffee. *Oh dear God, I am not going to make it.*

Before he leaves, our "messenger of death" presents Scott a white business card on which was written a name and a phone number other than his own—*Chris Nisbet, Dorchester County Coroner*—the county where my son's life, and my life as I then knew it, ended.

I hear the click of the back door close as the Greenville County Coroner departs, leaving me, Scott, and Susan in my kitchen. I lie down from the waist up and again stretch my torso across my kitchen island. "No-God-help-me-no—this–cannot–be" is all I can proclaim, over and over and over. My face burns. My eyes are already past swollen from too much salt in too many tears of disbelief. I feel like a helpless baby bird, mouth wide open, straining. No sound escapes. Scott mutters that we should call Clarke's dad. Before she takes the opportunity to leave, practically following the coroner out the door, Susan sadly assures us that if there is anything we need to just call.

As she disappears down our street, my brother-in-law Tom pulls into the driveway, according to the prearranged arrival time of 5:00 p.m., just minutes after the coroner leaves our home and a permanent mark on my life. Tom is loaded down with fixin's for the planned gathering—cocktail paraphernalia and potatoes for baking. My sister is meeting him at our house. Our plan all along has been to grill out, have fun, and watch football. Tom, who can't help but see and wonder about the white-shirted stranger who is driving away in front of Susan, locks eyes with mine as he comes through the back door. Confused, Tom asks, "Hey, what's goin' on? Who's that guy?" I look at him, unable to speak. I hear Scott from the background tell him. Tom's face turns ashen, and he drops his head. I walk over to Scott who is also crying. I can't speak. I fall into his body and renew my uncontrollable sobbing. Scott offers, "Do you want me to call Clarke's dad?" "No," I whisper as I stand trembling. "I'll call him."

During the next few minutes that seem like hours, I muster the strength to dial Carl's number in Myrtle Beach, SC; he answers with a chipper, "Hello" as if expecting a familiar voice—a pleasant call. "Hey it's me. I have … I have … I have something horrible to tell you. We just found out that Clarke was killed in an accident. It happened this morning." Dead-shock silence is broken by my cries of "Oh my God." Carl cannot understand my broken words. He interrupts, "What?" I struggle to repeat myself between breaths. Carl starts to cry in a high-pitched wail. *"NO, NO, NOT MY BOY, NOT MY*

BOY?' I can feel the phone shake and tense in his hand at the same time—no matter that we were over 240 miles apart at the moment. My knees buckle. I do not think that my legs can hold me much longer. Carl, in shock yet trying to maintain some sense of the here and now, raggedly explains that he had just been talking to his dad and thought the incoming call was his dad phoning back with a P.S. "I've got to go," his voice pleads and slowly trails off, "I need to call my dad." "Wait," I blurt out, "are you alone?" "No, a friend is here with me." Good.

My brother-in-law Tom thinks ahead and manages to call my sister Terri en route. By the time she makes her way to the house, she knows. Terri drags herself into the kitchen, grabs me, and begins to shake violently from the horror and disbelief of it all. I look down at myself. My shins and feet are still streaked with black potting soil. I still have on my yard shoes, shorts, and ratty tank top. My hair is still pulled into a rubber band on top of my head. This longest day of my life is dirty, smelly, and has left me stunned to where I forget to care. I ask Terri if she'll take me to my bathroom and help me shower. I don't think I can physically or mentally do it alone. I hobble back to my bathroom, using her shoulder like a crutch.

Meanwhile the phone is ringing off the hook, pleading to connect. It is incessant. I say to Terri, "At the back of my closet is Mom's old shower seat that she used a while back in rehab. I need it. I can't seem to stand up." Terri turns on the water and positions the seat directly under the showerhead. I sit on it, lay my face into my hands, and let out a wail that ricochets from wall to shower wall. Now it is I who shakes with no control. I can't turn my head, or even lift a washrag without feeling total despair. *My son is gone. Dead. He has been since before 10:00 a.m. this very morning. Not only had I been unaware,*

I had been unable to stop it from happening. We do the best we can, my sister and I. Despite our mutual state of delirium, she dries my hair, and we find clean clothes for me that actually match. It has been a half hour since the coroner left my house. *Thirty minutes, 1,800 seconds ... forever.*

It is now 7:00 p.m., the same day Clarke has died. Terri and I walk back into the kitchen as I suddenly catch sight of several people outside my front door. Remember, *everyone* has known since early afternoon—everyone except me and my husband, Scott—due entirely to a yet undisclosed and most unfortunate confusion at the accident scene and the extra time it has taken to set the record straight. In absolute grief and disbelief, friends congregate to comfort us, and as I now understand, to also be comforted. But no one can soothe me. The only thing that can console me—in this entire world, in this universe, in the heavens above or the hell that is now inside me—is to have my precious son back alive.

Chapter 10

From the foyer window, as the sun is setting, I see that the "several people" has grown to become a line of close friends all appearing at my home in hopes of attempting to discount this news they've heard. It can't be true! Dozens of young high school and college kids flank my yard; cars are pulling up and people flinging their doors open, not even bothering to turn the ignition off, and running to the front door, the back door, and to each other. One by one they make their way to Shadowbrooke Court. Everyone is crying; in my lifetime, *better I have gone a lifetime without seeing this,* I thought that I would never know a circumstance or a moment that could cause such sadness. As I open the front door, the mother of one of Clarke's closest friends is in front of me. We go to the same church. I'm frozen on Carol's face; every muscle is pitched downward as she tries to dam the flow of tears. She is unable; she grabs me tight and we cry together, as though holding on to one another will postpone the letting go of Clarke. I pull away from Carol and say with clear and emphatic resolve, "I need our Pastor David. And I need him *now.*" Carol immediately drives to Pastor David's house, interrupting his evening, his prayers, his personal plans, whatever. She delivers him to my front door in less than twenty minutes, later telling me she couldn't even remember getting into her car, much less driving to our pastor's house and back. She says, "Stephanie, it was like someone else was driving."

Pastor David, who, oddly enough is in *his* "yard work attire", steps with holy resolve into my foyer. I look up. In high school and college, Pastor David was a basketball player. He stands about 6'7". Within minutes, Pastor, Carol, Scott, and I form a tight circle. We pray while holding hands. "Heavenly Father, help Stephanie and Scott with this tragic news. Comfort them as only you can." Inside my head I hear the screams: "Why?" "No! It really didn't happen, did it?" But the armor of shock that cocoons me now begins to also act as a compass. I am being given emotional direction. To this day, I don't remember much of what I felt at the time because my emotions were wrapped within layers of impenetrable protection. For the instant, for my own good, my feelings are kept away from me. I am functioning on autopilot, fueled by adrenaline and propelled forward solely from my body's defense mechanisms. Unable to feel sure of my faith at the moment, *I am hoping ... praying ... pleading that somewhere in this darkness God is truly with me.*

I retrieve the white calling card from the kitchen while Scott and Pastor David talk about the service—some kind of meeting on Monday to discuss arrangements. Scott has always been great with details, and it's a good thing. He handles every morbid decision, from this moment and for the next two weeks. As soon as he and I are alone, I motion to our bedroom in the back. With card in hand and Scott at my side, I place the call to the Dorchester County Coroner who has my son's body. It's approximately 9:00 p.m. on Saturday. The day my son died.

Chapter 11

Chris Nisbet answers, hesitantly. I tell him who I am and he immediately launches into a thorough explanation of what occurred on I-95 this Saturday morning. The way he describes the unfolding of the incident is unbelievable, tragically bizarre. He explains the accident in this way: When called to the scene, Chris finds Brett's wallet near Blake, and Blake's wallet tucked in Brett's trouser waistband. The reason, we will never know. In reality, it is Blake who is still alive and who is rushed to the Medical University in Charleston, South Carolina, and put on life support. Based on the juxtaposed positions of the boys' wallets, his incorrect summary to the coroner in Greenville is that Blake has died at the scene with Clarke, and Brett is still alive but on life support. The Greenville coroner now calls on the homes of Brett and Blake, telling their parents the horrible news—the hearing of which would be tragic enough without having to hear it twice, in its erroneous entirety. In the meantime, a good friend to all three boys has received his cell phone alert about the accident and makes a beeline to the Medical University in Charleston. I cannot imagine how he must have felt walking into the intensive care unit. He knows that two of his childhood friends are dead *(only not the ones he thinks are dead)*. He stops short of the ICU door and takes one, shocking, "Oh my God!" glance into the room. Overcome with confusion, he quickly and frantically runs to find someone in charge and announces, his voice shaking and broken, "That's not Brett in there. It's Blake."

Now there are three coroners involved in this heartbreaking confusion: Chris Nisbet, at the scene in Dorchester County, and the coroner in Charleston who must now call his counterpart coroner in Greenville County to say, "There has been an identity error. You *must* go back to the two houses and correct the report to the first two sets of parents." Mind you, this all must take place before this same Greenville County Coroner can proceed to our house to tell us about Clarke. Consequently, I am told of my son's death a little before 5:00 p.m. Because of the mix-up at the accident scene, I learn that Clarke—the light of my life, my son, so full of surprises and promises—has been dead seven hours when I receive the unthinkable news.

I listen to Chris Nisbet against a background of my own primal moans, soft and barely audible. There is a youthfulness and compassion in his voice as he drops his direct manner down a slight notch and says, "Mrs. Benbenek, Clarke never knew what hit him."

Oh my God ... no, no, no, please don't say this to me if it isn't true! "Are you sure of that?" I cried.

"He was in his seat belt. We had to cut him out. He died of head trauma, but I can tell you that he went quickly."

"Oh God, you have him there with you?"

He replies, "Yes ma'am," and then proceeds to tell me of Clarke's exact injuries. The front of his skull was fractured, and he sustained a deep laceration on the back and base of his head. There was a lot of blood in the vehicle; it can only be assumed that it was Clarke's because the other two boys were thrown from the SUV.

To this day, I can't say enough good things about Chris Nisbet. His phone number and the man attached proved to be my temporary lifeline. I call the number this very night, the next day, and the next two days after that. Every time I call Chris he answers the phone with a noticeable hesitancy.

When he knows it's me, he relaxes a bit. After a few calls to him I remind myself of the thankless task of being a coroner, and that when Chris receives a phone call, it is always tragic. It is a death call. So of course, he always answers his phone expecting the worst. God bless these messengers of death. I know that Chris had to be thankful once my calls dwindled down. (Has a parent ever called this many times?) But I have a need-to-know type of curiosity, and Chris answers all of my questions in a professional and factual way, yet with a genuine kindness. A tragedy like this is incomprehensible; what can this coroner possibly say to explain all this to me? All through this same week, Chris faithfully visits Blake at the Medical University in Charleston. Then, six days after the accident, Blake, the only survivor, dies just after midnight.

Oh my dear God, where are you? The one thing that I cling to from the conversation with Chris is that Clarke didn't linger and suffer. Clarke died quickly. I actually am thankful and keep repeating it over and over that evening. As a mother, it is all I have to hold on to. It is a cheap white Styrofoam life preserver, but it will keep me floating until tomorrow. He didn't suffer, he didn't know what hit him, and he went quickly. But what about us? Those of us whose lives have imploded are suffering beyond what we think we can possibly bear. I couldn't realize at the time that the suffering had not even begun.

Chapter 12

The autopilot gears continue to turn. People are coming into our home to pay their respects. To console and be consoled. There are friends and family who must be called. The news will shatter their world, as it has mine, and for a brief moment I think, "If I do not call or tell anyone, it will not have happened. If a tree falls in the woods, and I am not there, does it make a sound?" Scott calls his best friend, a doctor in our city, and I say desperately, "Tell him to call me in something, anything to help me sleep. Something to take the pain away and get rid of this horrible visual that Chris had described. Whatever will work ... I need it."

My sister Terri begins calling family members from her cell phone. All of the words exchanged are hushed and somber, then loud laments of mutual grief for all of us. On the other end of the calls, loved ones fumble and release their phones in disbelief, too distraught to grasp the notion or the news. Several drop to their knees, screaming. Many hang up, unable to speak or form words or sentences. For the most part, every reply is practically incoherent. Terri leaves for the drugstore to pick up two prescriptions, one for anxiety and one for sleep and both for me. She returns, and we sit on my screened-in porch in a vertical fetal slump.

From the moment we hear about the accident this evening, everyone is taking turns picking up the phone as it rings, answering the questions no one really wants the answers to. My dad is attending his fiftieth high school reunion in Abbeville, SC. Terri calls one of my brothers, Chuck, who lives closest to Dad. Upon hearing about Clarke, Chuck somehow makes his way to the reunion event, pulling Dad out of the festivities to tell him in person of his grandson's death. Because of his heart bypass surgery in 2004, this is the only way my father can be told, for fear of his physical response.

Terri and I continue to sit, unmoving on the screened porch, hoping that a cool breeze can possibly carry all this away. We are whispering, shuddering, and crying in denial of the day's events when we hear a knock on the back door, the one that enters through the garage. Terri goes inside, and the couple who lives two doors down is standing in front of me, in the coming dark, loaded down with bags of chips and cakes, breads and sandwich stuff, and possibly a dozen cases of soft drinks. All the husband can do is just look at me and shake his head. His son and his grandson are both baseball players. Since Clarke had played high school baseball, we'd had that in common and would often stand out in the yard and talk for hours about the state of the game in today's world. This now silent friend came to cheer for Clarke and his team on many occasions.

Neither one of them attempts to speak. They just look and shake their heads, their eyes welling up. They come in wordlessly, unload the provisions, and just as wordlessly they disappear. Until that moment, I had never been around people who did not have to say a word. The lines in their faces told me more than words; *we cannot imagine your pain.* No, you can't. *If you need anything, anything at all ...*

Chapter 13

I am desperate for sleep, and the medicine my sister picked up at the pharmacy is the only way. Lying in bed and crying, my thoughts are on tomorrow when I will have to open my eyes to a world without my beautiful Clarke. How can I possibly gather the strength to do this? In my mind, a visual thought of Moses and the Red Sea enters my space. I begin to feel the fear and panic of the hopeless desperation that is crashing down on me, crushing my body with the weight of a million gallons of tears. I remember that tomorrow is Sunday, and ever since I could talk and toddle, I knew what Sundays were for: all about visitin' on church day. I squeeze my eyes tighter. I finally achieve a fitful sleep, holding hands with Scott.

In an instant, my mind transports me to my childhood. The oldest of five spitfire, rambunctious kids, I learned early that it was useless to protest Sunday visitin' whether it meant seeing relatives who lived in the same county or those who lived two plus hours away. Right after church, we would head out for the afternoon; all five of us sprawled in the back of our '69 Ford and each claiming their territory—on the back window dash (my favorite), on the seats, and on the floorboards. For kids who had far more energy than restraint, this was torture. Then, driving back Sunday evening and while my younger brothers and sisters slept, I would look into the sky out the back dash window and talk to the big cream moon.

Yes, tomorrow is Sunday, and to me and most Southerners, it usually means one thing. There's going to be a mess of dreadful visitin'. When I wake up I am still holding Scott's hand. It's Sunday, 8:17 a.m. Lying still, not wanting to become conscious, I watch a beam of sunlight daring to sneak in from behind our blinds and land ever so lightly on top of Scott's head and his pillow. Why is it that I am allowed to see and feel the waking of another day and my son cannot? My son loved sunshiny days, fishing, and the beach. Hot tears stream from my eyes. Like a hospital patient paralyzed, I feel like I can move my eyes only left or right to signal in the direction of what I need. Trapped in my body, trapped in my bed, trapped in my total despair. I know unwaveringly that my rational thinking is inside of me, aware of the goings on but powerless to do anything about it. I know that I am being protected—ironically by that same rational thinking—even though, right now, all I can do is open my mouth in a silent scream. One day I know that I will come out to face this vile thing that has occurred, but right now, this moment is all I can possibly handle. I cannot think in advance. The crushing weight of Clarke's death is too much.

Chapter 14

How life can change with the passage of one day, one instant. Saturday morning I certainly wasn't my usual self, but now, Sunday morning, I know that I will never be my usual self again. *Please, God, let me go back to yesterday morning. Please.* What do I need to offer? What will the universe demand of me to correct this horrific mistake? Cease this torture: ask and I will give it. My life instead, please? *God, why did you let this happen? Goddamn yourself. You screwed this up, you did!* Barely sixteen hours have passed, and it feels like a decade.

Now conscious, my awakening shocks me back to the events of yesterday. Like a bolt of lightning. Reality. I remember, as the Greenville County Coroner opened the door to leave my kitchen. I looked at his back and noticed that his shirt was actually too small and that the white cotton fabric had created, out of necessity, white horizontal pleats down his back going from shoulder blades to thick black belt. Every guy I ever knew who chose work in the field of criminal justice was usually the muscular type.

It was then, after the closing of the door and the coroner finally leaving that this feeling of being in a glass jar—like the lightning bugs we used to catch when we were kids—wasn't a glass jar at all. It is my body's natural instinct to shield me from this trauma. In a glass not delicate or hand blown, but sturdy, like Mason jar glass. The same kind of glass that protects God's sweet, ripe red tomatoes, grown last summer and put up in the pantry for winters to come. It's a glass that preserves the tomatoes forever because they're sealed airtight and nothing can contaminate them. This is how I come to feel: The glass I believe to be constantly surrounding me is a metaphor for my armor of shock. It has risen out of my very being and is protecting me from this horrible thing that will change my life and the lives of those I know for the rest of our earthly time.

Chapter 15

With tremendous effort, I crawl out of bed and without forethought, pour myself a cup of coffee, grab my cell phone, and call Pastor David. I desperately need to talk to him. I feel the suffocation and utter confusion of "not understanding." I dial, get his voice mail, and leave him a message. Pastor David has a sermon to preach; between his message reflection time and church service, he returns my call. I take the phone outside and find myself in the same patch of yard where just the day before my world ended. It was in this very place that I became surrounded by my glass jar. The phone interrupts my trance.

"Hey, Stephanie, it's David. I got your message. Is there anything I can do?"

"Pastor David, I … I … I …," and then the sobs begin. I continue, "I can't get my brain around the thought that Clarke has been taken from me because of my life, because of things that I have done in my past." Then I can't control it, and I begin to cry full throttle.

His soothing voice calms me. "Stephanie, no, no, our God is not like that. God is merciful. He did not cause this to happen. Our God is a loving God. Stephanie, it was an accident."

"Are you sure?" I croak.

He replies, "I have never been more sure of anything."

I wish I felt that sure.

I go inside my house, open the notebook by the telephone, and write. "Today, the circle of life is a black hole." This day will be like no other. I already know this, but I just have no scope, no barometer with which to measure just how unlikely

I will find it. And so it happens with a body of water. One day marine biologists measure its depth at two miles, and then something earth moving, even life changing happens. The bottom shifts, and the measure sinks to even greater depths. The branded question seared into my consciousness: "How deep can a body go? How sad can a mind be? How broken can a heart become and still beat?" Certainly, in this situation, sad enough that I would give my own life to try and seek the answer to my question, "Why?" Three small letters that form this most sorrowful and echoed word. Why?

Chapter 16

Were it to be like any other Sunday, this day would be a laid-back-gettin'-ready-for-the-week kind of Sunday. But today, less than twenty-four hours after the accident, we are absolutely stunned. Scott, normally creased, starched—certainly at the very least presentable in any circumstance—is totally not together. He is in wrinkled shorts and a shirt, shirttail out, and house moccasins. I am in a place that somehow (only God knows how) understands that things need to be done. I will do these things, but I will do them unwillingly. Scott calls the funeral home for me and begins setting up the "arrangements." Clarke's dad will be here soon and also Clarke's godmother and my best friend, Holly, both my sisters, my aunt from Texas—too many to think about, but thinking about it gives my mind somewhere else to go. Anywhere but the place where Clarke is dead.

Once again, I call Chris Nesbit, the Dorchester County Coroner. He confirms that Clarke's empty body is en route to Greenville. *Oh, my angel, I am not with you. But somehow I know that* YOU *are with* ME. The one thing that I *do* know is that seeing my son's body without his spirit is not an option for me. I do not want to see him lifeless. Clarke, forgive me for I am weak. Instead, I will remember you from six days ago, when you—now so mercifully—came home for the Clemson game and we had you here with us for twenty-four hours. So full of spirit and life. I will relive those memories forever in my mind. How I watched you sleep, for just a few minutes, before waking you up to go meet your buddies for the game. How you were with me that Sunday, just a week ago. Just us. Scott and I change into our visitin' clothes, and true to Southern tradition, the first vehicle now pulls into our cul-de-sac. It is 12:02 p.m. The "Sunday after" has officially begun.

Chapter 17

A mammoth navy blue SUV takes the opposite side of the cul-de-sac. It's Susan and Preston Reid. Preston has been battling colon cancer for the best part of this year. He has endured several operations, radiation, and chemotherapy. When Clarke first found out that his "roomie's" father had cancer, he yelled at the top of his lungs, understandably to reduce the pressure and deal with the unfairness of it all, *"MOM, THIS MAJORLY SUCKS! WHY DOES THIS HAVE TO HAPPEN TO SUCH A GREAT FAMILY? THIS IS EXACTLY WHY I MAKE MEMORIES, MOM. THAT'S WHAT IT'S ALL ABOUT ... PERIOD."* As I stand at my front window, an egg-shaped lump forms in my throat and my mind whispers, "This sucks ... why does *this* have to happen to my family?" Preston and Susan Reid have five boys; each are graduated or currently attending the Citadel. Their youngest, Kelsey, was Clarke's roommate second semester, freshman year. They had been fast friends. Kelsey's older brother, Patrick, was a member of Citadel's elite Summerall Guard and Clarke's captain on the school rugby team. Patrick and Kelsey emerge from the back of the SUV. More vehicles arrive at the same time; I see members of Clarke's Charlie Company. Several of the boys are in uniform; grey wool, black corded striping, gold buttons, and white pants. There, in the middle of the cul-de-sac, the young cadets meet up with the Reid family. En masse they are fortified for the worst. They make their way to the front of the house. I already have the door wide open to receive their sorrow.

As Preston slowly walks in the front door, weakened from chemotherapy treatments, he is followed by a row of silent ducklings—these big strapping Citadel boys. I say boys because at the time of Clarke's death, most all are nineteen years old. Preston used to quip, "I like to have my entourage of these big guys because no one messes with me as long as they're around." All of the boys take a step forward to comfort me, but it is either too late or too early. I am not quite sure. I know that when I look in their eyes and they in mine, we recognize such ragged pain that words are really unnecessary. It's the type of grief that is whispered over and over, in corners, on front porches, almost incoherently and in the saddest of voices. *This can't be true, can it?* We all feel the same way: helpless. It is some sick trick that we aren't in on and not soon enough, the trick will be over. Back to the way it used to be. I knew it took a lot for Preston to be here. It touches me immensely and even more so as he slowly musters the strength to ease into his well-known repartee for the benefit of everyone already gathered here.

Justin, one of the only other cadets in Charlie Company taller than Clarke, has arrived and is also in uniform. His eyes are unfocused and unbearably sad. I know immediately that he is in "that place." That place where I am. Far away from my body. *Like a dying man, that place, for right now, is the only way to survive.* He grabs my shoulders and hugs me tightly. I cry through closed eyes, my head on his chest. For a moment, I convince myself that this young man *is* Clarke. I plead to God, *Please be Clarke. Please be Clarke. Please be Clarke.* When I open my eyes and look up, it is still Justin. My tears stream down the front of his jacket. I never realized until now that the gray wool of the cadets' uniforms is water repellent. The tears bead down the fuzzy blue gray wool and end at the sashing of his belt. He settles into his grace, and asks, "Miss Stephanie, may I polish Clarke's brass for his dress uniform? I want to do it." It is too much. Justin is referring to the showy, traditional dress uniform of the Citadel cadets. It is to be, of course, Clarke's burial clothing. How many times had Clarke himself polished his own brass before early morning inspections? *As I'm sure he did the morning he died.* To Justin, this is a request of the highest honor. I shake my head yes, because I can't speak. I have to hold it together the best I can, every minute a new battle to be fought. I remind myself that we have to meet with the funeral home and Pastor David the next day, Monday.

Because Brett, who died at the scene with Clarke, will be buried September 14 at 1:00 p.m., we schedule Clarke's service for the same day at 3:00 p.m. A lot of the cadets have been given permission to come to Simpsonville for the funerals, and most want desperately to attend both services. The third cadet in the car, Blake, is still alive. Unconscious, but alive. Clarke's father will be arriving any time. Other close friends from Charleston, Atlanta, and Hilton Head are due in, and Clarke's paternal grandfather, aunts, uncles, and cousins from Pittsburgh and Virginia will be getting into town tomorrow. Then, there's all of my family—my sister Susie and brothers Chuck and Tony. Clarke's grandmother from Pittsburgh is too arthritic to travel; she is pitiful in her immobile anger. Clarke's maternal grandmother (*"Mimi" to all her grandchildren)* is in a local nursing home since suffering a massive stroke five years ago. But you can bet a dollar to a doughnut that Mimi will be here, stroke or no stroke. She may have lost her body, but her mind is still clicking. And all the other people who simply must come, unwilling to sit in their dens watching football or golf like any other Sunday. Come they do—by the threes and fives. Groups of grief.

Chapter 18

Almost everyone that I know, and certainly that Clarke knew is aware of my relationship with my son. Close cannot describe us. Perhaps symbiotic would be the better term. One of us would bring topics up, and the other would say, "I was just thinking of that," and then we would talk about it. He and I could butt heads, but we always connected. We were honest with each other, and to tell you the truth, he was more honest than I. I had decided a long time ago that there would be secrets and stories about my coming of age experiences that I would take to *my* grave. My friends and I used to laugh about it. I'd say, "Lord, girls, don't tell your kids everything about you, 'cause they'll use it against you. They will throw it in your face and then what can you say to them?" Clarke knew I wasn't perfect, but I just never told him how imperfect. But I really was honest about life—about what to expect, who you could trust and how you should treat people. Then there were the coming changes in his body that he was not to be ashamed of. The teenage experiences that had already happened and those yet to happen, we talked about freely.

Chapter 19

Could there ever be a longer Sunday in my life? People coming by the houseful to pay respect to Scott, to me, and to Clarke. Friends floating, almost unconsciously in and out, leaving photos and mementos of Clarke: friend, coworker, nephew, son, grandson, and teammate. And oh, the heavy shroud of sadness. A conscious realization finds its way into my brain; this is very well the first time these folks are experiencing the death of a child. Both a friend of their children *and* a child of *their* friend. As they file through our home, I try to identify one person who has lived through a child dying. I come up empty handed. Not one. I will tell you this with certainty; our friends and family would have done anything, short of sacrificing their own child, for this not to have happened. I see it in their eyes. What I mean is that people literally would trade at least a limb or more; the older ones, their very life, to have the circumstances reversed and Clarke back with us. Everyone seems to wonder when I will collapse.

The phone, constantly ringing. A notebook by the main phone line in the kitchen is used to log messages and what people bring to the house. Clarke's rugby coach, Major Bill Bell, and Lieutenant Colonel Pamela Barton, his TAC officer at the Citadel, call to offer up memorable anecdotes when Clarke first started playing rugby the year before. I am not quite ready to hear these yet, but I half listen and half smile out of respect for the effort. First Battalion commander at the Citadel is arranging for the cadets and the Regimental Band to have bagpipers at graveside. These details take at least five phone calls. The commander says about seventy cadets from Charlie Company are coming to Clarke's service. "What?" I swell with pride in spite of the very reason that demands their presence. "And Mrs. Benbenek, next week there will be a memorial service here at the Citadel in the Summerall Chapel. I'll get back to you with specifics." My head is past spinning. I feel like I am in a vacuum, powerless to do anything except hold on and survive another hour.

The dining room is a hub of activity. Boxes of pictures are brought out and ruffled through, with the chosen photos used to create two collages for the visitation and for the vestibule at the church. A sister of one of Clarke's best friends joins in this valiant project out of respect and love for Clarke. I am sure she is thinking the entire time, *this could be Chad. This could be my brother.* She's preparing a Power Point presentation for the celebration service on Wednesday, attacking the project like Joan of Arc leading a crusade. It will be the finest job she's ever done. The poster board collages and the video presentation consume this group of friends until the very day of Clarke's service. They work tirelessly. The boys choose music to put with the video. Together we select five wonderful songs that Clarke loved: "Something to Be Proud Of" by Montgomery Gentry, "Myrtle Beach Days" by the Embers, "You've Got a Friend" by James Taylor, "Red Dirt Road" by Brooks and Dunn, and "Forever Young" by Rod Stewart. Later, one of the boys calls me to ask about choosing between an additional two songs. We actually converse about the merits of each, and then we agree on one. *My God. Wrap your arms around me. I will slip into nothingness unless you protect me. Can anything protect anybody?*

Chapter 20

There are three journals out for guests at all times. One of the boys' moms has seen to that. I offer no resistance, so she just runs with her plan to be a help in organizing the chaos. So many people come in and out like a carousel of compassion. *(This must be some bizarre test of my sanity, a theory I keep rolling over and over again. Surely there are drugs powerful enough to put your mind in this type of trance. My center of gravity is shifted. Everything appears to tilt slightly amiss of linear. As I am being pulled off my painted pony, I am hanging on for dear life. You need to get off, Stephanie! I want to scream. This cannot be real. But it is real, and I have no choice but to stay on, holding onto the moving pole until my knuckles bleed.)*

And then there are all of Clarke's friends—vibrant, invincible young men and women whose world has been stabbed by the reality that death is not something that just happens to grandmas and grandpas. One of their own has been taken. The unfairness of it all. They run into my house and collapse in my arms, shaking uncontrollably, professing their love for Clarke, for me and for each other. We all know that Clarke's smile could feed the masses. He could multiply it and then multiply it yet again. He was adored by his girl friends and his guy friends. He made them laugh. He talked with them in a thoughtful way. He did not judge his peers. He felt compassion. He was loyal and reliable, and he loved to go and do. These are the friends who now turn to me to anchor their sorrow to any type of bobbing security. They come in packs—young men who practically knock me down with their physical sorrow and girls that I must literally hold up because they cannot stand.

Jon, Jay, Kim, Jonathan, Kevin, Andrew, Kemp, Leslie, Ryan, Hunter, Chad, Eric, Bailey, and Kelly. I catch a visual of Brett Rice in his tattered Mauldin High baseball cap with both hands on top of his head, like a prisoner of war, looking upward with tears streaming down his face, saying over and over, "I love that kid, I love that kid, I love that kid." Too many to remember each part. I know that I will never forget the total impact.

I am going to have a nervous breakdown, except for the fact that I don't have any nerves at this point, or maybe I am just one big gigantic nerve, taking the brunt of it all to the point of numbness. I am really not sure of anything. I think maybe my nerves have shriveled inward for protection, and my emotional side is operating autonomously. Or maybe my emotions are shriveling, and my nerves are taking over. Either way, it is the only way that I am able to withstand the onslaught of grief that has begun and is yet to come. I ask Jonathan and Andrew if any of the boys might want to speak at the service, and without hesitation, they answer in unison, "Yes." I will ask Pastor David the next day and get back to them. Little do I know that Clarke's close knit group, or, as this group of Mauldin High School graduates liked to call themselves, the "Mauldin 7," after leaving our house, will hold a candlelight vigil this Sunday night, lasting well into the next morning. Together, these remaining six friends will compose what they want to say about their friend, Clarke Russell. They choose Andrew to be the spokesperson.

When Sunday is finally said and done, Scott estimates 350 people have come through our doors, 351 counting my aunt who arrives from Texas late evening. Adrenaline kicks back in to carry me until after midnight. I don't need food. I don't need rest. There is only one thing I need, and I will drop from exhaustion or death before I will ever have what I really need again.

Chapter 21

*I have quickly concluded that having to deal with a funeral just a day or two after your loved one dies is obscene and unbelievably cruel. How can one even think through the cloud of sorrow and shock, much less make **decisions**?*

Yet here we sit, early Monday morning—me, Scott, and Clarke's dad, Carl—talking to a funeral director. He hands me a zip lock baggie. In it is a debit card receipt and three folded $1 bills. I smile. Scott actually chuckles out loud. Only our Clarke would be heading out of town with $3.00 cash. In the past, he amazed us with his frugality. If necessary, with his personal money, he could be as Spartan as a monk. But if it was our money or if he received some extra birthday cash, he definitely treated himself.

"Where are my son's clothes and his other things?" I ask like a marionette, my mouth hinging open and shut. Is this my voice? I am speaking but I am not conscious of the words. The director looks at me and says, "I will have to check. His clothes were very soiled, and you know, blood is considered a biohazard. The embalmer has to exercise caution." I stop him with a fierce glare. I feel Scott tense. "It's not your decision," I say, starting to feel hysteria creep up my backbone. "If his things are covered in blood, then it is my blood and my problem to deal with. It is *my* blood," I repeat sadly. The car, what was left of it, was in a garage area in Charleston. In that car are Clarke's things: his civvies bag, his phone, his wallet (things that were not Clarke, but they were his). I want to touch the items that were on him, near him, with him, when he died. With concentration, the funeral director writes a note to himself to check on the clothes in which Clarke died. I have to push this problem away for now to deal with the details of the present.

The director continues with his rehearsed spiel, "What is Clarke's Social Security number? Did he have any hobbies?" *These questions make me want to retch. Why the hell do you need this useless information? I want to grab his somber tie, nose to nose, and scream at him to quit asking these trite questions. MY SON IS DEAD! Do you not get it?* Now we are standing and walking to a room filled with caskets. My legs may not hold. Satin and silk pleats, titanium, copper, steel, wood, fiberglass. Does it really fucking matter? And how about these guest registry books that cost $120 each when you can go to a bookstore and get the same for $25? But I am mute. It hasn't been nearly long enough to deal with this. I wave a dismissive hand to everything. One of teenage girls' favorite words—*whatever.* Scott weighs in on my behalf, and he and Carl pick out the casket as well as the vault of thick steel in which the casket will be placed. *Protection. Protection, I cry, why? What does steel protect my baby from now?* Several other funereal items are offered, but this is when I throw my hand across my throat in a slashing motion to say, "Cut it, we are done. Let's just get the hell out of here ... *now.*" I am, quite simply, out of my mind with grief. Out of my mind and out of my body. "Oh, one more thing, Mrs. Benbenek—we will need the obituary by 4:00 p.m. today for it to make the Tuesday edition of the newspapers."

Chapter 22

As we turn onto our street from making the funeral arrangements, we see the cars that already line our cul-de-sac on both sides; I open my back door to a kitchen full of friends, some I have not seen for months, even years. They have been gathering in my absence, waiting, refusing to leave until they see me. The looks on their faces, the width of their open arms, their utter disbelief, and their incredible emotion wash over me in buoyant waves, holding my soul above the water. They gather around me in a circular way as if to shield and save me. From what, they do not know. Only I know, and I don't know nothin' yet.

Early this afternoon, Scott and I meet with Pastor David at the church to discuss the service, or as I keep repeating, the celebration of Clarke's life, rather than the devastation of his death. It is a private meeting. Pastor, Scott and me. We talk about my Clarke, we laugh, we cry more, and we hold hands. I can't stave off the tears. No matter how hard I try, they just keep flowing from some bottomless font deep within me. Pastor David says, "Firstly and most importantly, let's talk about Clarke and God and what is happening spiritually right now. Stephanie, there is no time and space. There is a thin veil between what was and what will be. Clarke is not waiting for you, looking at the clock, aware of elapsed time. In his world, it is just a moment before you will be with him once again." I find comfort in Pastor David's words. He continues, "Stephanie and Scott, sometimes I have to really try hard to fill a service with good things about someone who has passed.

With Clarke I am going to have a time of it, keeping the service from going on for hours."

We continue to talk about happy things, about how our house was a gathering place. Constantly concocting salsas and sweet creations that I cooked for Clarke and his friends because I wanted to. Because it filled me with happiness, just as it filled them with the same and then some. My specialties took on their own identity. Steph's special salsa with a kick, a plate of pickles and cheese were Polish appetizers, and then there was doo doo dip—don't ask for specifics—and of course, plenty of Brats, burgers, and chicken on the grill. I would come up the stairs to their "boom boom" room—their moniker—with trays of goodies, constantly interrupting their robust video games, using food as a ploy to try to engage them in meaningful conversation. Wrong. Clarke would yell "Mom! We're in the middle of a competition here. We'll all come down and talk to you later. Please scram!" "You'd better," I would say as they attacked the food. And they always did come down and talk with me. Then they'd herd out to go home, shower, rest a bit, and then start socializing from house to house. Huge groups of them. Almost all of the time, I knew where to find Clarke. In the middle of his peeps' posse. And everyone knew that you couldn't talk about Clarke without talking about his love affair with a mirror. I constantly chided him for checking his image in every mirror he passed; if a mirror couldn't be found, reflective glass would do just fine.

Pastor David recounted to me and Scott how, during several youth group retreats, Clarke would ask very insightful questions about the *why*s? and the *how*s? of life. He told of several conversations in which he and Clarke exchanged spiritual points of view. With one hand, I am holding on to

Scott for dear life; with the other, I am wiping my tears, blowing my nose, discarding that tissue, and pulling a new one out of the box at my feet. I know I've gone through at least twenty. When our voices trail off as if there is nothing left to say, Pastor David asks us to pray with him. For the thousandth time, I close my eyes, hoping that when I open them none of this will have happened. Next, he will reflect on all that we have said and craft his message for Clarke's service on Wednesday, day after tomorrow. I don't realize until much later just how strong Pastor David was this day. Knowing me, knowing Clarke, knowing us together, how can anyone not be affected?

I ask Pastor David—upon the condition that they are willing and able—might some of Clarke's friends speak at the service? "Absolutely, that will be great." Scott and I leave, with hopes and dreams in the air, words hanging—spoken and unspoken. I know that our lives will never be the same. The heat of the Southern sun in these dog days of summer feels strange on my skin. I am spent for the day, for the year, for the rest of my life.

Chapter 23

We return home, mute. I can't seem to even form a sentence. Scott and Clarke's dad decide to go to the cemetery to purchase the plot. As they leave, Holly, who has been staying at the house, looks at me and says, "Steph, you need a manicure and time away from the madness." I acquiesce. I look around for my other friend Barb, give her my credit card, and say, "I need two black dresses. You know my size. Please go buy them for me." Holly and I get in her car, *no way I can drive*, and she takes me away, if only for an hour. At the manicurists' shop, I lay fully down on the waiting couch; everyone else will just have to find another seat. I close my eyes. I am hungry. I am exhausted. I am numb. But still so much left to do. Tomorrow night, Tuesday—visitation. Wednesday—Clarke's service.

By the time Holly and I return from our manicure, Scott's car is back in the driveway. He and Carl have bought the small piece of earth that will hold the body of my child. There is also a big, black, chrome-plated truck parked at the end of the cul-de-sac; all of the cadets are in an assembly line, unloading Clarke's things that they had so graciously offered to bring home from the Citadel. I am surprised at the speed at which they'd unpacked his dorm room and returned back to us.

Clarke and I—okay mostly me—had worked so hard to organize and pack for the new school year just over three weeks ago. *Only three weeks!* Gray plastic bins precisely labeled and marked with Sharpies: *CLOTHING, DESK/STUDIES, PERSONAL*. Uniforms ironed and folded.

In the front yard, Carl is watching this solemn act of dedication and honor. His arms hang limply on his 6'6" frame.

He reminds me of a massive scarecrow that is in bad need of new straw. He hasn't the strength to pick up a pencil, much less a box to help these boys. He cries like a child. I know Clarke's grandpa, aunts, and uncles will be arriving later this afternoon. For me, they can't get here fast enough; Clarke's dad desperately needs some tender loving care, and I am too overwhelmed with my own sorrow right now to care for anyone else.

I lead the way upstairs and ask the guys to just stack everything in the "boom boom" room. Today, there is no raucous laughter here. No salsa, no Polish appetizers. I know there never will be again.

I continue to limp through this Monday. The thought of the next two days seems to be just a tiny swell way out on the horizon of the Atlantic Ocean. But soon enough, I will be caught under the wave. As it arcs above my head, I will be helpless to do anything about it before it comes crashing down and pulls me under. The endless stream of friends, neighbors, and family does not stop. I beg someone to close off at least one of the entrances to the house so that we can stem the flow down to two lines. Common sense. *How the brain continues to function when it has been disconnected, I don't know, but it certainly reinforces the concept, to me anyway, that there is more at work within us than the body and the mind.* In the ensuing months, I come to intimately know the meaning of spirit, soul and willpower.

Each chime of the doorbell announces more plants and flowers to cover the floors, the hearth, and every available ledge not already laden with food. Every spare surface in my large kitchen and dining room is covered and overflowing. Defensive moves are in place before refrigerators can be opened, lest stacked items come tumbling out. I know that most come with a heart for comfort, but as always there are a few who simply come to see how "the family is holding up."

Chapter 24

Newspaper articles, online messages, a Citadel Web site, and the funeral home Web site are information links through which people from all around the world are communicating with us, in sorrow and in grief. Our computer room becomes the hub of all this information. We are set up with cable Internet and have a pretty good fax setup as well. A "Caring Bridge" Internet site has been set up for Blake—his condition continues to be critical. Messages from everywhere are reaching his family, too. Since the accident, he has not regained consciousness. Everyone waits, watches, and prays, helpless to do anything else.

Blake's mother calls us from Charleston. She has been in the ICU of the Medical University of South Carolina nonstop since Saturday. "Blake is going to make it, Stephanie. He is going to make it for Clarke and Brett. We are praying for you." "I am praying for you, too," I say. Her voice sounds strong, but I can't help but wonder if she is jelly inside. Her call is meant to give me hope, but my hope is hollow. Frequently, I find myself on caringbridge.com to check Blake's progress, bow my head, and press my hands together in prayer. If I press hard enough, maybe the strength and energy from within me will come out through my fingertips and shoot straight up to the heavens. In my head, over and over I hear from my childhood days and from Clarke's days as a young child "... *if I should die before I wake, I pray the Lord, my soul to take.*" Somehow, knowing the extent of Blake's head injuries, in his mercy, God will call his soul. Yet if one person can survive this tragic accident, it might restore some bit of faith to my bleak heart. Like her phone call to us, Blake's mother's messages on the Web site also seem confident and upbeat. As numb as I am from Clarke's death, I can't imagine the torture of knowing and seeing that your child is barely alive, teetering, and you—helpless to pull him back. Back to your bosom, to hold and shush and soothe him; maybe sing him a soft lilting song to let him know it's going to be okay. Mommy's here; everything's going to be allright.

When Clarke was little, I would lie in my bed at night and pray to God that I would live long enough to set him on his path. The thought then of not being able to grow old with him was devastating. The knowledge now that this will never happen is too much to comprehend.

...keeping Clarke.

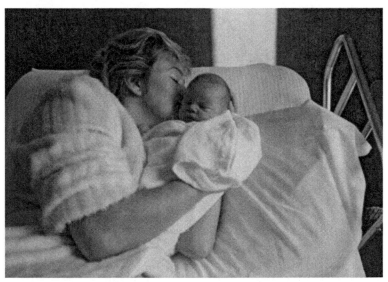

...keeping Clarke.

Chapter 25

After Clarke's accident came out of nowhere striking me like a 300 mph freight train, the fact that I am still standing is a miracle. Scott says it best, "It's like you've been hit, and your body is still intact but your insides are, well, a train wreck." Following an emotional trauma such as this, something happens to you physiologically and on a cellular level. When all of your natural defenses rush in to insure your survival, likewise, your cells must shift to make way for these "soldiers of shock." I know to let them through. For at this moment they are meant to defend—helping at a time when I am unable to help myself. As time progresses, my cells slowly shift again ever so slightly, yearning to resume their former position within my body. Truth be known, they never quite make it back to the exact spot or to the exact function they performed before the tragedy. I am now and will forever be altered from my original person.

I grew up hearing from grandparents and great uncles and aunts that, in the old days, surviving a tragedy such as this, a person would become nothing more than an empty shell. It was proclaimed to be an expected state of insanity. *Ever since the accident, she's been crazy as a loon; she's not in her right mind; one day she just left us; the light went out and never came back on again.* This is probably closer to how I am feeling. I was so sure that if anything, God forbid, ever happened to my child that I would surely die. Well, it is two days later with a visitation and a funeral staring me dead eye down, and I am still alive. I don't know how it is so, but it is. The only reason I can fathom why is that I have an obligation to fulfill. *God, please help me to keep my mind.*

Chapter 26

I speak to everyone who is in my house—twenty people, at least—and then I excuse myself. *It is time.* I sit down at my office desk to write Clarke's obituary. I have until 4:00 p.m. this Monday afternoon. Words want to come through the stem of my brain, but their flow is clogged, unable to find a passage out. I never thought that I would be writing this. *This! This! This! My darling son's obituary*—my mind screams, *"THIS IS NOT RIGHT!"* "I know it's not right," I lash out, "but who else can do this other than me?" *Nobody,* I answer back in a whisper. Over the course of all time after Clarke's death, that same voice will continue to ask over and over again, *"Who will do this? Who will stand, who will live, and who will speak for Clarke?"* *The answer is always the same. I will.*

I cannot start. I sit with pen in hand, motionless, not knowing what to do. I have never written an obituary before. Somehow I get the first word on paper, then the second, and then the hundred more. It is now the eleventh hour and I am on the phone with the funeral home secretary asking her to read back to me what I have just sent her. It's about eight minutes past my 4:00 p.m. deadline. I do not want a picture. I can barely eke out the facts, as they are. What are the facts anyway? The obit column just makes the next morning's edition of cheap newsprint. My entire life reduced to a column in the "Upstate Deaths" section. My son's life—a mere recollection in print, when all I truly wanted was for everyone to remember Clarke as I do, the Clarke that only six days prior, had come home for Labor Day weekend—my beautiful boy: happy, self-confident, the physical embodiment of everything young and strong. The public visitation will be Tuesday night from 5:30 to 8:00 p.m.

Chapter 27

Clarke G. Russell

Simpsonville

Clarke Gibért Russell, of 308 Shadowbrooke Court, Simpsonville, S.C., born on January 6, 1986 was instantly called away September 10, 2005, by his Heavenly Father.

He did not even have time to say good-bye to all of those whose lives he touched. Clarke gave his family and friends an abundance of love, laughter, and unspeakable joy. Those that are blessed to have known and loved Clarke will carry his spirit in their hearts forever.

A 2004 graduate of Mauldin High School, Clarke's love of tradition led him to attend the Citadel where he was a member of Charlie Company, "The Casual Cats," the Citadel Rugby Team and had just begun his sophomore term.

He is survived by his mother and stepfather, Stephanie and Scott Benbenek of the home; his father, Carl E. "Caz" Russell of Myrtle Beach, S.C.; his paternal grandparents, Carl E. and Genevieve "Honey" Russell of Belle Vernon, Pa.; maternal grandparents, Charles M. "Gandy" Cape of Myrtle Beach, S.C., and Hazel G. "Mimi" Cape of Greenville, S.C.; and a multitude of loving aunts, uncles, cousins, and friends.

A service celebrating Clarke's life, officiated by Pastor David Taylor, will be held Sept. 14, 2005 at 3 p.m. at Eastminster Presbyterian Church, 2240 Woodruff Road, Simpsonville, S.C.

The family asks that in lieu of flowers, donations may be sent to The Citadel Foundation, in memory of Clarke G. Russell, 171 Moultrie St., Charleston, S.C., 29409.

The family will be at the home.

Chapter 28

Several times during the day I check on Blake's progress, hoping each time that something different, something positive has happened. It hasn't. Many of the cadets and most of our hometown young people have lost two friends, with one still fighting for his life. Soon, within hours, the cadets will leave their hospital vigil in Charleston and drive to Simpsonville to attend Brett's and Clarke's services on Wednesday. They will also attend a school memorial the next week at the Citadel's Summerall Chapel. So stoic, these brave young men and women. How do you disseminate a senseless tragedy like this? In their world that is so ordered, so basic and military in nature, how do you possibly make any order after an unnatural order of events that has turned everyone's world upside down and inside out?

In the overall scheme of things, I feel like I know very little of what happened to my son on September 10, 2005. What I know, or think I know is very simple. I know that he is gone. His physical body is lifeless and empty. I have to take something for sleep in order to stop the racing strobe and the visuals of the accident I conjure up in my mind. My body, my heart, and some of my sense of rational thinking are firmly encased by my shock armor. Tomorrow at the funeral home, and then the next day at the funeral, I will have to hold it together as best I can. And then the day after that. And the day after that. My darling Clarke would expect it, no, demand it from me—just as he always encouraged the strength of his fellow cadets and friends, he would plead for the same strength from his mom.

Later this Monday evening, just two days after the accident, the flow of people dwindles from en masse crowds to two or three per knock. My friend Barb produces the black dresses I requested. Check. Holly commandeers the kitchen. Check. One of my sisters continues to help Clarke's friends make picture collages to display at the funeral home. Check. My other sister is acting as taxi to other family members who have arrived at the airport. Check. At 10:00 p.m., just when I think I might finally be able to sit, more friends drop by. Good friends. So I visit a bit more with Jake and his dad. Jake is the young man who screamed attention to the identity mistake at the Medical University in Charleston. His father, through tears, says that his younger daughter can't come, she is so angry at God. We all sit at the kitchen table and cry. Jake and I share some special memories of Clarke, and he tries so very hard *not* to share his tears with me. Then, with a heaping plate of food, they go. I can't help but think that they go home, alive and well, and that my child is dead.

Months after Clarke's death, it was on an overnight visit to Charlotte that Holly looked at me and said, "Steph, I can't believe that you're not angrier with God." I paused and before I even knew how I would reply to her statement, I said, "I have been very angry that God didn't perform a miracle and save Clarke's life, but with Clarke's injuries, I've come to believe that God did perform a miracle by letting him go. It was an accident, and I know that Clarke would not have wanted to live if he couldn't be Clarke." And that's the truth.

Chapter 29

These past two nights are mostly dreamless. Normally, I'm a very vivid dreamer, down to a colored paisley pattern on a necktie. The past two mornings I only remember dreams of red and black slashes, bold and feathered out like angry strokes of a painter's brush. *I am sure that this emotion is chaos trying to overtake me completely.* I am even more certain it will be the same dream when I wake tomorrow, Tuesday.

Anyone who wants to know about the accident can easily go online. *The Charleston Post and Courier* first runs the story on Sunday, September 11. Today, Tuesday morning, September 13, a full recount runs in Greenville's newspaper. The headline, "Friends, family cushion loss by celebrating cadets' lives"—and the reality of visitation later this afternoon—both come with my morning cup of coffee. You see, you still somehow, without any basis or sound reasoning tell yourself that maybe it isn't real. As if your strength in denying it may make it not so. *If you have the faith of a mustard seed, doesn't the Bible say that?* I vacillate between reality and fantasy, suspended by a fine wire of disbelief. The gravity of what has really happened is pulling my line so tight that at any moment it could snap, catapulting me, tissue-thin emotions and all into an even deeper pitch. No words can describe how I dread what lies ahead. I talk to one of the Citadel faculty members again by phone; I need to confirm the funeral times for those cadets planning to attend. Again, the house fills with friends and relatives, all milling and mulling around aimlessly, speaking to each other, studying and touching the many items that remind them of Clarke. I was asked and gave an emphatic "yes" several times to, "Miss Stephanie, is it okay if I go up and sit in Clarke's room for a while?"

The boys come by to get my approval on what they have written for their part in the funeral service. I tell them that it's not necessary for me to read it. They are shocked; very rarely did they know me not to double-check everything. With Scott's help, I delegate as much as I can to those who have offered. It's a correct assumption that getting dressed and showing up is all that I need to do, if I can only try and stand up and get through these next few days. After that I will collapse and pray for something—anything that will make my thoughts and my very being disappear. Until then, I have got to hold it together. For Clarke.

Chapter 30

Monday and Tuesday and for weeks afterward, a load of envelopes is removed from our mailbox each day and deposited in a large basket. I cannot even attempt to read these cards. By reading them, I will give credence to their purpose: comfort in the time of death. Each postmark and potted plant serves to strip away the veneer of fantasy that this might not have actually occurred. I start to think back in my lifetime and remember who, of my acquaintances and friends, had the most foliage in their home? *Were they the leftovers of a funeral?* I couldn't remember.

Apparently something I say makes no sense at all. Scott looks at me and says, "Did you take something?"

"Why?" I ask.

"Because you are slurring your words."

I can't believe he is honing in on such trivial bullshit. I look at him and say, "Scott, I am speaking slowly because if I don't I will scream, and I will not stop." I continue to stare at him. "Do … you … understand … this? And, yes, I took something because we have to go to the funeral home and stand in a line and actually *greet* people!"

"Okay," he says. I know that he is worried about me. He still can't fathom all that has happened, either.

I get dressed in one of my new black dresses appropriate for visitation. Tired, swollen and red, my eyes barely resemble what they normally look like. Waterproof mascara. Check. Eyeliner. Check. I go through the machinations of becoming presentable, somewhat normal. Every breath, ragged. Every step—a major task. I don't think I can do this. Maybe this is when I *will* lose my mind. Maybe this is when *my* light will go out. I will begin to babble and scream and not make one single lick of sense. The psychiatric police will have to put me in a straitjacket and transport me out of the funeral home. *That would be fine. Thank you very much.*

It's close to one hundred degrees outside. Scott and I are in the bathroom—combing, spraying, sighing. As we prepare to leave for the visitation, Scott snaps me back to the present and says, "I've never experienced such an outpouring of kindness and love like this ... ever. I want to tell you that it has changed my life." I nod in agreement, because I can't speak. I want so desperately not to have my Clarke be the reason for his miraculous change.

Scott and I leave for the funeral home around four twenty-five. Plenty of time to get to where we need to be, right? Wrong. Even though it's only fifteen minutes to downtown and we've allowed ourselves one hour and fifteen minutes, there's an accident on the parkway, and we're stuck in traffic for almost thirty-five minutes. By the time we pull into the funeral home parking lot, my skin and stomach are twitching, and I would give anything for a paper bag. *I really just want to vomit.*

Chapter 31

Nothing I can imagine, no presupposed scenario that plays out in my mind—not even one movie of the thousands I have watched could prepare me for what takes place over the next two days, and for many days thereafter. Scott and I enter from the rear of the funeral home, through dark, old wooden doors. We walk alone on well-worn, Victorian–designed carpet, passing by a murmuring, peaceful fountain. How many had walked before us on this same path? Clarke's maternal and paternal families are gathered in the visitation room. We all form a straight line and stand before a plain, pewter casket covered in roses the color of bright blood.

I am conscious of the closed casket, but I don't want to look at it. I have put my blinders on, and I am here to do the job that Clarke would want me to do, albeit in continued total shock. I feel like a girl in a picture waving and smiling at the camera, totally unaware of the cliff drop off behind her. The two collages that Clarke's friends had worked so hard and so lovingly to prepare are positioned on an easel. I look down the hall leading up to the casket and see an endless line of people. As my eyes scan the human sea, I lock eyes with no one but connect with everyone. I walk, wordlessly, to the collages to look at the photo images of my beautiful son. Then it is time for Carl, Scott, and me to take our places in a receiving line next to Clarke's aunts, uncles, grandparents, and cousins.

I turn to accept the tears, the sorrow, and the embraces of a line that winds around the outside of the funeral home onto the asphalt parking lot. In unbearable heat, people shift patiently from foot to foot waiting to pay their respects to my son and his family—some for four hours. All in all, almost five hundred people come to see us that evening. I hug every last one of them. I know this because the next day I cannot lift my right arm. Old friends from sixteen years ago show up, having come into Clarke's life when he was only four years old. Clarke's teachers back to kindergarten, coaches and friends. Distant family members consistently saying, "I bet you don't remember who I am." Most of them I do remember. It's incredibly overwhelming. A young cadet steps up and says, in a broken voice, that he was down in Tallahassee for the football game, setting up the tailgate when he got the news. He breaks down and throws his arms around me. Entire sobbing families surround me, huddling as if we are all here to select the game of life's next big play. But there are no more plays; the clock has run out. All I can do is receive the outpouring of love that engulfs me and hold it together the best that I am able. Here we stand—the shell-shocked lot of us—in front of a casket that holds the empty body of Clarke.

Chapter 32

I want so very much to open that space and crawl into the satin pleats with Clarke and be one with him again. *My baby. I bore you and fed you and held you and loved you more than my own life. I have praised you, defended you, and punished you. I have taken out your splinters and taught you that life is not always fair. I would give **anything** if it were me in the casket instead, with you standing so tall and handsome in your dark suit, receiving our friends and family. Believing and saying and praying over ME, NOT YOU.* "My mom was a good woman. She had a good life. A husband she adored and loved. Yes, I loved her so much. Her grandchildren will miss her terribly. Oh gosh, yes, I know how proud she was of me." Clarke should be alive. I should be dead. That is the natural order of life and death. I glance down at the unending line; occasionally seeing heads cock out at an angle to the left to estimate how much longer it will be before I am in their arms. And they in mine.

After the last of the respects have been paid and the tissue boxes lay empty all over the funeral home, my friends Holly and Margaret leave the funeral home to grab something to eat; I imagine more as a respite from all the emotion instead of real hunger. In a short time, Scott and I will now be alone together at our house for the first time since our world was thrown into reverse three days ago. On our way back home, a friend who's in from Atlanta for Clarke's funeral calls and asks if it's okay to stop by. *Of course you can stop by … why the hell not?* Scott and I have the rest of our lives to be alone.

Scott and I visit with her for a couple of hours and then go to bed. I wish with every altered cell of my altered body that tomorrow, September 14, will not come. So powerful is my longing—I imagine while I sleep that a massive and successful nuclear air strike is about to obliterate the United States. It is the only way I can hope for any type of reconciliation with God. Clarke has died so he will not have to suffer the horrifying effects of radiation. *I ponder like this, not that God caused the accident to happen, but rather that he did not step in and intervene with a miracle to save my son's life.* I am certain that I will awake tomorrow to a wasteland of charred earthly remains. Black pillars of salt and smoke. Right now, these thoughts are the only way I can imagine ever forgiving my God. That and the one other saving grace: Blake is still alive.

Chapter 33

I love the mind and body exercise of yoga. Move your limbs deliberately, gracefully, as if you are in slow motion, as if you are moving through mud. One of the basic principles of yoga is to forget the past, not to worry about the future, and to live in the present moment. I start to feel this way about living with shock. Every exertion, although painful, is deliberate and isometric; I concentrate my efforts to give my mind someplace else to go. *Slowly make your way to the large white rectangle in the kitchen. Reach, reach your hand toward the opening handle device, stabilize elbow, tense forearm muscles, wrap fingers around bar, and from stable elbow, pull to middle joint of palm. This is how I open a refrigerator.* Now, my eyes scan each item on each shelf—you get the picture. The minutiae of each effort are a sequential order for everything, even the simplest of chores. It is the only way I can stay above these churning waters of total chaos and disorder. The pyramid is balancing on a needle, upside down. This is not the way the world is supposed to be.

I catch myself pausing in whatever I am doing and becoming very still. I use the strength of my will and hope that a revelation comes upon me, the unfolding of a higher purpose through the death of my Clarke. I look to the skies and find comfort gazing at clouds, searching for divine answers, and praying for revelations. Doesn't that cloud look like a young boy running? Is that the word "love" written in wisps of white air?

So much of my life becomes almost robotic. I start to count and add everything, become obsessive about it actually. Every number is assigned a meaning. Clarke died on 9/10 10+ 9 = 19, the age at which he died. It seems meaningless yet bursting with meaning all at the same time. The number of days that he lived was 7,192. Add them up. They equal 19. It seems that every time I glance at a clock it reads 6:16, the exact minute that Clarke was born. What do these things mean? Probably nothing. But they mean everything to me. It's like anything that we can associate with the one that we love is so important.

Chapter 34

On the day my son is to be buried, I awake to the roaring sound of nothing. I feel an innate connection with the First Mother who lost a child. It is here that I find my deepest understanding of my loss as Clarke's mother. In my mind, I conjure earth as the First Mother knows it. I imagine the child that caused the first smile on the first mother's face. Before words can be formed, before there is language on our planet, there is a mother who has lost her child.

No fear, these ancient ones. Wearing and eating what they have killed to survive. Mothers warm in fur dress from hirsute animals and who only know *right now*, this moment. A scream from deep within a winding cave, echoing off the walls of rock and carved stick figures, searching for the opening to lance the well of unfamiliar feeling inside, to breathe the air. The earth is all the First Mother knows. The earth and a nameless force, the spirit of something other than herself. The Maker of booming clouds and cleansing rain. When the cold comes and the forests become small, she, her protector, and the little ones that have come from within her go through great hunger and thirst. She braves the creatures and the elements to protect what is hers. Like the night's white guide.

But while the First Mother cannot question, she instinctively understands one thing; everything she knows and is has come from the life-sustaining earth. We are born from the earth; we go back to the earth. Mother Earth. Yes, she has seen the bodies of others with no air, whose eyes are closed. But when the clods of earth cover the body of *her* child, she wails. What is she feeling?

She is feeling her own death. She is feeling the acknowledgement of love and loss. She knows that the beat in her chest is the same cadence as that of the beat in her child's chest. The two are one. Even Mother Earth cannot separate them.

For that child was born from inside the mother, and the mother has given part of herself to the child. And the child will be welcomed into the earth as the mother welcomed the child. The mother will someday join the child. But for now, this moment, the pain of a million mothers before me who have each mourned the deaths of their children has settled in my heart and in my soul. So I too must mourn and cope with the death of my child and also with the death of my life with the one I loved so. I will never wake a whole person again. And only when the mother joins the child is the absolute pain set free to continue its journey. Today, I am the mother, and pain begins its sojourn inside of me.

Chapter 35

Briefly optimistic that indeed our world was destroyed overnight while I slept, I hear the air conditioning unit click on, feel a mule kick me in the gut, and realize sadly that the world is the same today as it has been up until today. The paper is delivered in its usual wrapping, full of old news and new sales. It is Wednesday, September 14. Half asleep, parents are shaking cereal boxes, smelling the milk in a container that expired five days ago and yelling, "Hurry, you're going to be late for school. No, I don't know where your white T-shirt with the green writing is ... I washed it and put it away yesterday. Now, for the last time (which really might be the fourth to the last time), come eat breakfast!" Not so long ago, that would be me and Clarke.

Struggling to clear the morning mist from my spent brain, I remember Brett will be buried today also. Once more I cry, "God, why didn't you save them? Why didn't you save my son? You know that by Clarke dying, I have died, too." Cruelly though, I haven't died. My armor of shock continues to send me across rooms to be comforted by arms that are attached to faces filled with curiosity. Each is wondering if I will make it through the void of life without Clarke and waiting for the other shoe to drop. *"Can I go on?"* *I plead with God, "Not, will I go on or may I go on, or I don't want to go on ... just a simple question of CAN I?" The reply is an echo of nothing.* Soon after the accident, Scott—trying desperately to keep me in the here and now—said, "I know you feel that life is over, but we have to go on. We have no choice, right? As hard as it's going to be, we have to keep moving forward." He always ends a question with the word "right?" if he really is not sure himself. He is afraid for me, he is afraid of life with me after this. Naturally, he is afraid for himself. I would visit his words often during the agonizing months ahead, and still to this day, the words resonate.

In this tragedy, I come to know the vast expanse of everything, the overwhelming power of nothing, and what it is to exist in the chasm between. To the best of my guessing, I have tumbled almost halfway down, but for now, my will to survive overcomes my wish to die, and I know that in this chasm of nothingness I must eventually find a new dimension of peace. That and a reason to open my eyes each morning. As a parent, of all the shudders we experience trying to keep our children safe from harm, I realize that up until now I have only felt the nick of this unending nightmare, never fully dreamt. In the months ahead, I will understand the decisions I will need to make to keep myself from becoming a free bleeder.

Again, true to Southern form, no one except immediate family comes to the house prior to the funeral. Three of my girlfriends agree to forego the service to ready the food and beverage for "after." Holly instructs them down to the last detail. Everyone performs their tasks in whispers and soft shoes. It is right at one hundred degrees by the time the black limo, with air conditioning a bit on the fritz, pulls into our cul-de-sac street. A crazy thought that Clarke would have thought it way cool to have a white stretch instead, enters and exits my head in the same instant.

Chapter 36

Hotter than forty hells and a funeral limousine with air conditioning that's seriously in need of Freon, September 14, 2005, is fiercely determined to be miserable in every aspect. Immediate family gathers first at the house, including my nephews with mementos of Cousin Clarke in hand. One nephew with a Pittsburgh Steelers knit cap, one holding a small French Huguenot cross, and both with a need to place these keepsakes with the casket before it is lowered into the earth.

We all leave the house together and arrive at the church; Pastor David directs members of Clarke's family into a side room to pray. Maternal and paternal hold hands in a huge circle. Every face, a stunned mask, unable to accept that Clarke is gone. The prayer from Pastor David is one of peace and strength. When Amen is voiced, my youngest nephew, just eleven years old and clutching the small cross for Clarke, bursts into tears. We are led into the sanctuary. Our sanctuary doubles as a basketball court, fellowship hall, or whatever the need dictates. We are not one of these fancy churches with the pipe organ and the gleaming wooden pews, carpet underfoot. Rather, it is simple and holds about five hundred people. Any more and they stream into the narthex, a greeting area at the entrance of the main sanctuary. The really pretty thing about our church is that behind the main podium area is a series of vertical windows that gives a beautiful view of varying shades of lush green trees and foliage in the summer, and in the fall, fiery oranges and reds. It is a very peaceful setting, and it feels as if you are looking at nature from a secret and secluded place, especially now in the dimly lit sanctuary.

Today, the casket has been placed at the front of the stage, backlit by the sun through the windows. The whole seating area is bathed in shades of grey and black; the casket spray of red roses reminds me of a colorized Turner Classics movie. It is, in fact, the only color I can see in a roomful of darkness.

Chapter 37

How am I going to sit here and not throw myself upon this pewter casket? How? I do not know, but a small inner voice commands me to maintain unbroken eye contact with both Pastors Tandy and David. God will empower them, and through them, I will receive the same. *Do not waver,* I keep repeating in my head. This, right now, is about and for Clarke. Clarke had heard me say many times, when something *had* to be done, especially a task that you weren't looking forward to or didn't have the energy to do, "Well, of course you can do it, son. You can stand on your head for twenty-four hours." This meant, in plain English, suck it up. You can do *anything* for a day. Today, this day, is my headstand.

The church is capacity and then some. The walls are lined with silent Citadel cadets, most from Clarke's Charlie Company. In rigid grey wool uniforms buttoned up to their Adam's apple, *in this heat for God's sake!* All with hats in hand, stone faced, and each having retreated into "that space" that they learn to go to for safety, for protection. The knowledge of this survival tactic starts with the freshman knob year, when cadets realize that mind control is what conquering the gruel of the Citadel is all about. They are in this place today. By contrast, Clarke's hometown friends, too many to number, are extremely vocal and demonstrative in their grief—girls and boys, men and women, sobbing and comforting each other. No one is immune to the resonance of loss we all feel.

So it is that it is ending and it is also beginning. As my eyes lock with one, and then the other, these two wonderful pastors conduct the celebration of Clarke Gibèrt Russell's life.

Chapter 38

The cemetery is just a scant quarter mile from our church, so as soon as the funeral service is over, the graveside service begins. I endure the burial on a day so hot, even the breeze blows fire. The relentless sun inhales the questions, and the heated exhale delivers no answer; it only dries all of our tears into salty streaks. A lone bagpiper from the Citadel, in full Scottish dress, plays "Amazing Grace." Why do bagpipes sound so sad, so plaintive? Clarke loved a bagpipe because to him, it exemplified tradition. Pastor David prays aloud and then the Charlie Company commander kneels in front of me and presents me with the folded Citadel flag. The funeral director motions for the family to rise and make our way back to the stifling limousine. I walk from underneath the tent and step on dry, beige grass, my heels aerating the hard ground. Not one person in the crowd encircling the tent makes a move to disburse. I am feeling my way, slowly, every brittle step, through this throng of silence. I stop and look at the limo driver, who's dutifully been standing by, and I say, "You all go. I am not leaving right now." No one says a word.

The air is still, and I wonder if I can get a deep breath. I feel that at any moment I will spin out of control and start babbling incoherently. At one glance, I look at everyone's faces. Then they all morph together, and I look at none of their faces. Suddenly they have become one sad countenance. I open my mouth to speak. I tell them how much Clarke loves them. I tell them I love them too. I do not have the words to express my sorrow or my gratitude. My attempt is feeble, but what is expected? My love, my light, my son is dead. I realize that my voice is not my voice. It sounds very far off, a light mew carried on the hot wind. Then circles of bodies come round, trying to comfort me by giving me any type of physical contact. As if by touching in some way, they will bring Clarke's body closer to mine. But no one can comfort me, although I do feel an overwhelming sense of love and sympathy radiating from everyone. Their fears, their doubts, and their collective *why*s? hover in the air. Silent prayers going to God, "Please take her hurt. Please ease her pain, Lord. Please show us a reason why this most awful thing has happened. For us, for Stephanie, for all of us that loved Clarke so deeply."

I can still see my nephew's small hands nervously tugging at the band of the Pittsburgh Steelers cap, pulling it this way and that, not quite sure when he should let it go. After the graveside service, *God, I hate the word grave*, he just tosses it on top, turns, and looking down at the ground watches his feet half run away. I wish I could run away, too.

Chapter 39

Back at the house, my body is floating from group to group. My family, Clarke's friends, Clarke's grandfather from Pennsylvania, Scott's coworkers, our mutual friends. I am only to wander around, and then around again. Revolution. Not the first time since this horror, I am again amazed at the autonomy of the body to go through the motions when you are dying inside. I block out a lot of what is said and most of what is done. Even those family members who are already hitting the sauce hard, I ignore. The reality that everyone deals with their own individual grief in their own individual way pretty much gives everyone a kitchen pass for indiscretion. Screw it—what can be worse than what we are going through? Everything else is petty, trivial, and of no consequence whatsoever. Soon enough I find out that the fine line between getting out of bed and lying in one's own urine is but a shadow of a line. It is so very difficult to keep from falling into a state where apathy is the normal order of the day.

My out of town friends will be staying until this Sunday, the eighteenth, the Citadel is holding a memorial for Brett and Clarke on September 20—the very thought of which sends me into a tailspin—and Scott is to return to work the twenty-first. This means that, soon this hive will become dormant; the queen deep within the honeycombs, withdrawing, so as to save what little energy she has left. Her humming, barely audible. Her wings, flailing as she buzzes angry signals. "Where is the honey?" she will ask. "Where is the honey?" In the combs, her prison, she can only spin around and around as the answer, once golden, becomes waxy and hard. "The honey is gone."

Chapter 40

The side server in our dining room becomes a treasure chest of memories. From the first time that I reach for the pulls and for a thousand times more, the deep drawers hold the precious mementos of that time before the accident. Instead of neatly folded linens and silver serving spoons, I store pictures, newspaper articles, and all the special items that friends bring by. Everyone's personal moments with Clarke—frozen in time on photo paper. *God help us all.* The many different parts of a young man's life. Boyhood—self-conscious and toothy; adolescence—sassy and skinny; teenager—confident and "badass." All the stages of Clarke's life in a never-ending loop of images. *"Why have I been robbed of knowing my son as the man he was fast becoming?"* The top drawer of the server spills down to the largest, bottom drawer. Each time it's opened and more treasures added, it becomes that much harder to close. Mounds of memories create a number of piles throughout the house. The basket of cards grows and overflows, but I am not ready to read the words intended to comfort. I know these heartfelt outpourings will only deepen my sorrow.

For the next several days while I have bodily reinforcements, I do mindless things. I ask one of my friends to help organize the flower cards so that "thank yous" can be sent at a later time. Holly has a notebook in which she has recorded the copious amounts and types of food that have been received. We laugh, we cry, and of course we hug tightly and frequently. All of this without conscious, cognitive thought. Their friendship and support is a nest where I am offered safety. I burrow there for the remainder of their time with me and welcome the process of not processing anything at all. I can't look beyond the next hour, much less the next day. It is with a desperate sadness that I say good-bye to them. They have normal lives that need their attention. I ache for that normalcy, for life before, but I know that I'll never have it again. As everyone drifts away from me and back into their routines, an overwhelming melancholy envelops me. It is with me every waking moment, and during sleeping moments, as well. Each morning the stain of my tears is on my sheets, my pillow, and my satin eye mask that I use to keep the light out; and whenever possible, the truth.

Then on Friday, just past midnight Blake dies and this accident becomes one of the worst multiple fatalities in the history of the Citadel, including all the majors: the Civil War, the World Wars, the Vietnam War, the Korean War and the recent War in Iraq. Three beautiful, vibrant young sons.

Chapter 41

I know Clarke would like this color. It's now Monday the nineteenth. Scott and I are driving to Charleston for the memorial service planned for the next day at the Citadel. Prior to our leaving, I go to a department store, find a salesperson, and say, "My son has been killed, and I have to go to a memorial." Through her tinted glasses, I see how my statement takes her aback. "Bring me whatever you have in any shade of blue that is simple and conservative." She brings several outfits back to the dressing room. Once again, sequential and robotic, I try on and dismiss several items, finally choosing a top and skirt in periwinkle—close enough to Citadel blue.

After slipping into the restaurant's cold vinyl booth that evening at dinner, I grab my mobile phone, dial a number, and then with a start, throw my hand over my mouth to muffle a sob. "Honey, what's the matter?" Scott asks, concerned. "I am trying to call Clarke," I cry. It is such a natural thing to do. I am in Charleston, and I have to call my son. The rest of tonight is a blur. I allow the tears to come freely so that somehow I can try to maybe, just slightly, dry up the reservoir. The last thing I want to do is cry uncontrollably at the Citadel service tomorrow. *God, I need sleep.*

The memorial for Clarke and Brett, scheduled for September 20 at 11:00 a.m., starts exactly on time. Of course. What else would you expect? Brett's family sits in the left side of the pews in the historic and beautiful, worn dark wood and brilliantly stain-glassed Summerall Chapel. Clarke's family on the right. The somber group of young cadets of Brett's and Clarke's respective companies, Lima and Charlie, file in silently and take their seats. Others from the school slide in the middle. The entire football team takes the back section. The Citadel Chaplain begins; both boys have friends wanting to speak, as well. For Clarke, it is Justin Weathers and Jon Griffin, two of the FAB 5 (FAB means Forever a Brother). Clarke made three, Kelsey was four, and Justin Heaviside totals five. That's Clarke's core Citadel group of best friends. Excerpts of their tributes follow:

"... I'm sure I speak for many when I say, 'the things Clarke has shown and taught us about life have changed our lives forever.' Although his time on earth was not as long as we would have liked, Clarke has made us better people by touching our hearts and teaching us a lifetime's worth of lessons. He showed me how to live everyday like it was your last ... He was the guy you'd go to when you were having a bad day and needed someone to lift you up ... I'd like to thank you for making us feel like a part of your family, and in Citadel tradition, you will forever be a part of ours."

Justin Weathers "Beak," Charlie 2008

"... Clarke to me was not just a classmate or a roommate—he was a best friend. ... his constant flexing in the mirror, that same familiar laugh and his famous saying of 'yeah, baby, yeah.' I don't think I ever recall anyone making sure that they had to say 'I love you' to their parents before hanging up the phone like Clarke did. After witnessing Clarke's funeral, I realized he touched a lot of people in his life. Clarke, you will always be missed and never forgotten. Going to miss you like a brother ..."

Justin Heaviside "Teeth," Charlie 2008

"When I first met Clarke, he was laughing ... we had just reported and he was laughing. I thought, this guy won't be laughing much longer ... but I was wrong. He continued and kept his smile all year. I like to think that when I have a good friend, I take a part of that person with me forever. Whenever I get down, I recall a memory of Clarke, and it always brings a smile ... Clarke's spirit will never die."

Jon Griffin, Charlie 2008

At the end of the memorial service, a lone bugler plays "Taps." The tears stream silently while I fidget with my tissue. I wonder how I have made it ten days. I know that I am still deeply entrenched in a place that is protecting me, and all I can do is simply thank God for it. After "Taps," the service ends and every member of Charlie Company files past us to pay their respect. Again, I hug everyone in this receiving line, and then Scott and I leave to make our way home. He is going back to work tomorrow, and for the first time, I will be walking solo through this wilderness of grief. I am sure Scott is worried about leaving me. Is there any possibility that faced with the emptiness, I will take my own life? I know the question is formed, but no one has the nerve to give it voice.

Chapter 42

After days of bouncing around my house like a small silver pinball, I begin to lose what little sense of connectedness I have. The phone rings, the mail is delivered, and people stop by to check and see, "How's Stephanie doin'?" It is very obvious, however, that as life continues chugging right along, Stephanie is on the tracks, suitcase in hand, waving good-bye. I have missed the train, and I don't know what to do. Where am I going to go? How can I possibly get there?

We return from the Citadel the evening of Tuesday, September 20, and Scott prepares to return to work on Wednesday. When he leaves through the back door, I know that just like everyone else, he will be going back to what is normal for him. But what, I wonder, will be normal for me? I am left with this void, a deep and ragged crater that hit me suddenly one Saturday and changed my entire world. I am fearful and totally fearless all at the same time. *I want to find the First Mother, the ground zero of this grief, to search countless caves, to hunker down and retreat deep within. Regardless of what anyone thinks, I will eventually come out, filled with the understanding that only loneliness can give you, and knowing that nothing will really ever change except me.* I will emerge, use my hand to shield my eyes, and feel my way along—squinting at the brightness of everyone else's life.

I try to straighten up the house doing so in a helter-skelter intermittent fashion. I imagine that a person with emphysema performs their daily duties this way. Walk to the desk, pick up a bundle of papers, sit down, and try to breathe deeply to gather enough energy for the next task— never completing one but always starting another. There are brown leaves on all the plants and wilted blooms on the flowers that had arrived in sympathy for Clarke.

I sit on the bottom step of the stairway that leads to the kitchen and think how many times Clarke had come bounding down these stairs—rushing in and picking me up over his head so he could show off his muscles and how strong he was becoming; me all the time, laughing and screaming "put me down this instant." His reply, "You need to quit eating bonbons and watching television, Mom." "What?" I would jump to protest, recounting all my nonchocolate chores and accomplishments of the day, and watching as a self-satisfied smile spread across his face. Gotcha! I can't count the number of times I was reeled in by my son. He always knew the exact buttons to push to get me going. And get us laughing.

I go outside to collect the nonstop stack of mail, although we already have multiple piles of sympathy cards we haven't even opened. I'm just not ready to read them. Then I realize, not quite consciously, that I may never be ready to read a card about the death of my son. Never.

Mail in hand, I return inside, sit on the hard wooden stair steps again, and begin to cry profusely, unable to form a thought. I reach for a small trash can, place it on the step beneath me and wrap my calves around it. I open junk mail and catalogs, toss them away, and find myself left with a handful of cards. For some uncanny reason, (*didn't I just say never?*), I pull just one out of the stack and begin to rip it open. I look at the return address on the small cream envelope. It is from a person I don't know. As it turns out, the sender is another mother, a friend of a friend. She expresses her sympathy for my loss of Clarke and then goes on to write about her sixteen-year-old daughter who was brutally murdered for the $10.00 her parents allowed her to carry. I sit staring at the note. I read it at least six times; somehow it eases my heart just a bit. As bad as it is going through the death of your child, there are definitely degrees of tragedy. Things can always be worse. How, I don't know, but this woman certainly does. I say a silent prayer for her. I also ask myself why I opened this unfamiliar card, especially when I have stacks of paper sympathy from those I know intimately. I feel and tell myself I opened it because, oddly enough, it was exactly what I needed here and now at the bottom of my stairs, at the bottom of my sorrow.

Chapter 43

Do I want to die? Do I, really? Absolutely. Could I have taken my own life? In a heartbeat. Would my son want me to choose this as my reaction to his death? Absolutely not. From that moment I stood in my grass, phone in hand, listening to a grown man sobbing in response to my query of "what is wrong?" I felt an immediate infusion in my body—a type of force that has no name or definition. I had heard about shock and read about it. In passing conversation I even would have said I understood it, when actually I didn't know squat about shock. Until now. With this—arguably the worst event a person can endure—shock has risen up and armed itself with a hammered shield and razor sharp sword. It stands over my deep valley, wielding its power not only for me but against anything that dares to come near me. I am in the lowest part of my valley's shadows. My God, shock is powerful: so powerful in fact that it stays the sentinel of my life for almost a full year.

But there is something else, too. That feeling you get right before the roller coaster takes its plunge—a lifting of the spirit, a lightness that makes you believe you can fly and places you slightly out of body. I believe with all of my heart that this inner feeling is God—that this is my faith awakened. I physically feel God wrap his arms around me and envelop me with divine insulation to keep my spirit and my soul alive. God and faith on the inside and shock on the outside. It's a safe bet that nothing will get in, and it will be a good long while before I get out. Thus begins my journey through the valley of the shadow of death. I skirt the precipice many times, just a breath away from falling in and away from those I love. The reason I am still here is that I believe I will be with my son again, *and* that the only true way to honor Clarke is to live like he would have wanted me to.

Chapter 44

For the second time in a month, Scott and I arrive in Charleston late in the evening Friday, October 13. I have been crying off and on for the past few days, dreading this return trip, but knowing in my gut that this is what we need to do, this is where we need to be. This particular Parents' Weekend, Charlie Company is planning a special tribute to Clarke and had invited us to participate. And while it is the Citadel's way of honoring Clarke, it also allows the cadets to grieve, and in the words of one senior administrative officer—"get on with their lives." This is, after all, a military-based institution. The cadets affected—*who wasn't affected?*—can't go on wandering about in a disbelieving stupor forever. The death of a friend is not an excuse to fail.

When we get close to the hotel, I say to Scott, "We have got to stop at a store. I need some Jackie Os."

"What the hell are you talking about?"

"You know what they are, big black sunglasses. A good pair will cover my face from the forehead to the middle of my cheeks." He started to make a protest until he looked at me, and then thought better of it. If I could get a little security from a pair of shades, then so be it.

We both know that we need a good night's rest for what this next day will bring. I can only hope to cry myself empty before tomorrow morning. As with Clarke's funeral and the memorial service in the chapel, I have to again draw strength from some part of me that I never knew existed before this tragedy. I am trying really hard to focus on how proud I have always been of Clarke and how much he accomplished in less than twenty years of life. On Parents' Weekend, while I realize I may never be a parent again, I know that I will always be Clarke's mother.

Promptly at 10:28 the next morning Scott and I enter First Battalion for the memorial for Clarke. Charlie Company displays a wreath made of every blue flower imaginable. Clarke's closest friends greet us, and one of them, Justin, hooks his arm and escorts me to show what has been done in Clarke's honor. The cadets have hung a large, white sheet from the railings above on the third and fourth floors. On the sheets are huge letters: *CLARKE GIBÉRT RUSSELL, JAN. 6, 1986–SEPT. 10, 2005 CASUAL CATS 2008 NEVER FORGOTTEN*. In the middle of the sheet is the Charlie Company logo, The Pink Panther, the most casual of all cats, painstakingly colored in bright pink from the top of his head to the tip of his tail? At the top of each set of stairs—starting at the ground level all the way to the fourth level—is a bulletin or chalkboard. On each is a particular drawing or slogan paying tribute to Clarke.

At the top of the second flight of stairs, which is where Clarke had lived, I stopped short, quite taken aback. My mind immediately shut down—another shock protection. There, resting on the floor is a small wooden cross on a square base, painted white with Clarke's last name in neat black, block letters. Resting over one side of the cross is a pair of white gloves, the type worn by all cadets during special formations. Positioned in front of the cross is a pair of spit-shined, black lace-up military shoes. The sight of this wood and leather tribute nearly brings me to my knees with sadness. This is what my son's life is now? A cross and a pair of shoes? *My God, please let me die. I only thought I could make it. I don't really think I can.* I can see by the looks on their faces that Clarke's classmates are very proud of their tribute. I reach behind me and find Scott's arm for support. I squeeze as hard as I can, releasing some of my tension into him. The door shuts in my mind, and I try to focus on what I need to do—make it through this. As we rejoin the hundreds who are gathered down on the main level, the commanding officer asks for the crowd's attention. He then proceeds to give a beautiful speech about Cadet Clarke Russell; how he will never be forgotten and how very special he was. Next, the company chaplain asks for a minute of silence and concludes with a prayer.

The red and white checkerboard inner courtyard of the main level is extremely crowded with parents, family and friends. There are only certain weekends that barracks are open. This is one of those weekends. You see, for the "Knob" freshman year, it's the first time that parents are reunited with the young men and women they had dropped off as boys and girls in mid-August. They've been through Hell Week and a healthy adjustment period to the rigors of discipline at the Citadel. I remember our Parents' Weekend the year before. Beaming with pride, so happy, so content. I couldn't quit hugging Clarke. He looked so handsome in his uniform. He was a man, so different from the boy we had brought to the Citadel. The goofy Clarke that Scott had said wouldn't make it two weeks.

I am relieved that Charlie Company has made their tribute to Clarke's memory *before* all the other festivities. That means Scott and I can make a beeline for the exit. No one would even miss us, and I am finding it increasingly hard to breathe.

I almost make it out of the courtyard of the barracks without totally losing it. Almost. I am taking a long last look at the white sheet waving good-bye to me, high atop the rails of the third floor's balcony. Suddenly I feel a tug at the bottom of my shirt. I almost chalk it up to being brushed by one of the many visitors here today. I feel the tug again. I turn around and at first do not see anyone. Then I look down. I'm not overly tall by any stretch of the imagination, but this woman is very diminutive—so much so that she is literally out of my sight line.

As I gaze at this small Asian woman through my black protective Jackie Os, she struggles to speak. She, too, is wearing big black sunglasses that look to be prescription. Tears are just beginning to streak her face from under her glasses as she points up with an emphatic little finger. It is obvious she knows very little English. It is hard to make out, but I finally understand, "My son, my son," as she stabs the air over and over. "My son make dat, my son make dat." She delicately gulps for air between her words. It takes me more than a few seconds to look in the direction of her finger. She is pointing at one of the sheets hanging overhead, the breeze distorting the big black letters of the message it carries. "My son make dat foh yoh son," and she continues crying and clutching her handbag, not really sure what else to do.

I realize it has taken much courage for her to approach me. After all, she hasn't a clue how I will react. Culturally, we are worlds apart, so she has stepped into the area that we have in common. We are mothers. That's what matters. She, like me, loves her son more than life itself. Then, I do precisely what any mother would do. I bend down to embrace her, she hugs me back hard, and that's when I lose it. Yep, I almost made it.

Chapter 45

There is a grief support group for those who are coping with the death of a child; I ask Barb if she will go with me the next evening. Maybe I can find some solace in the company of others who truly know the misery of what I am experiencing.

There are thirty people and then some, all sitting around the perimeter of a meeting room of a local church. Some in this grief group are holding hands. The junior high church basketball team is practicing in the gymnasium one floor down; the laughter and thump, thump, thump of the basketballs bring memories of Clarke rushing through my brain.

Each person takes a turn and tells a story of his or her child's death, the circumstances, how long it had been since the death, how he or she is trying to deal with it. As I repeatedly hear, "It's been eleven years. It's been eight years. It's been six years," I can't believe it. Each month, these people gather and relive the death of their child, and some have been doing it for years! My inner thoughts are reeling. I can't picture myself sitting here month after month, re-experiencing Clarke's death. I will go stark raving mad. I realize right then—*what I really want is to celebrate Clarke's life*. If I remain frozen in the moment of his death, I know that I will not survive. *I must try to relive the multitude of moments before his death.* For this feat, something this monumental, I know I will need professional help. A therapist and a lot of courage. I have to make a connection with someone who's equipped with grief experience. Because I can't do it alone.

Chapter 46

I begin asking friends for recommendations for a therapist. *Anyone know a good miracle worker?* I spend one entire morning calling a list of names. Each phone call is torture. The instant I start to say, "I need some help. My son was killed in an accident," I start to sob uncontrollably. In gasps, I blurt out the details. I make my first connection with a grief therapist on October, 21 and my first appointment is set for Nov. 4. I didn't hold out much hope, yet strangely, I couldn't wait for my first session.

Like a bully (who isn't really a bully at all, but rather, a frightened child lashing out on an unfair world), I swagger into Teresa M.'s office. With both anger and resentment cocked and loaded, I challenge her with several pictures of a beautiful and smiling Clarke. I sit on the sofa and immediately sink down six inches where innersprings used to be. Then I spit out my words, "Unless you can bring my son back to life, you can't help me." I stick my chin up, readying for the punch, and when it doesn't come, I begin to sob in long ragged gulps. She sits there and without taking her gaze from my face, reaches behind her and produces a box of tissues and hands it to me. I can't speak, only catch my breath, blow my nose, and renew my sobbing. After about ten unabated minutes, she begins to speak to me in a very soothing voice, almost too low to hear, "I know you are experiencing incredible pain right now. There's nothing that either I or anyone can do to bring your son back. I simply want you to know … this is a safe place for you to release your emotions, no matter what they are."

Teresa resumes calmly. "When you go through a trauma like this, all of your reactions, whatever they may be, are normal." Can this be true? Is the rush of wild and irrational thoughts normal? *Jealousy of those whose children are alive, apathy, panic, avoidance, suicide—normal?* Is the silence of no feeling and total numbness on the flip side, *normal?* I think silently about her words. With my sobs hanging in the air, I demand, "Did this really happen? Dear God, what am I going to do? I just don't know if I can live, if I want to live ... how in the hell am I supposed to live?"

"One day at a time," she says. Somewhere down below, beneath my armor of shock, I choose a different scenario. I open my mouth and say, "One hour. One hour at a time." "Very well then, this hour has passed and you've made it. Would you like to schedule another appointment?" Several years later, I can say with certainty that therapy did help me. It helped me to understand what a human being goes through—physically, psychologically and emotionally—when faced with the unimaginable. It helped me look forward and embrace the "imaginable," in a way I never thought I could. Our sessions over the years also taught me—directly and indirectly—lessons about life after death. None of this would have been possible without the work on my part, choosing to live as my son would want, opening my heart, and stepping out in faith. I began to look at life again, not in the way I did before Clarke died, but in stages. One hour at a time.

Chapter 47

I think I was in the first grade, second at the most. The buzz around school was the upcoming solar eclipse. As a class, we were to meet all of the other classes outside at the predetermined time and place, ready for the event. Once outside, the girl who sat next to me in our classroom stated with confidence, "The sun is going to turn black and disappear." I didn't like the sound of that at all. "It won't really disappear, will it?" This thought filled me with dread. As a youngster with an active imagination, it didn't take me long to imagine the worst. At the time, we had recently come out of the Bay of Pigs standoff with Cuba. Later on, we sat solemnly at our desks as the principal announced the assassination of President John F. Kennedy. The nightly news had started in me a fear of nuclear attack.

"Well, it might disappear for just a little bit," the girl quipped as she jumped up and dug her shoe toe into the dirt to make the merry-go-round go round. "And then it will turn cold and we'll all die like the dinosaurs!" she squealed, and then we both started laughing. Our teacher said sharply, "Boys and girls, come here quickly, time to get our equipment ready. Now, let's take our milk cartons and make our special eclipse camera."

I had washed my paper milk carton out at home, cut the top off, and dried the inside so that it magically could be turned into a camera with which to watch the solar eclipse. "You can't look at the eclipse!" my classmates chimed in excitedly. "Your eyes will burn up and you will go blind." So we each took our milk carton and covered the open top with tin foil and taped it down good. We cut a flap into the side of the milk carton, pulled it back and away, and then used a straight pin to punch a hole in the taped up tin foil cover. Immediately you could see the small concentrated beam of light reflecting through the pinhole onto the bottom of the carton. It wasn't the whole sun, but it was all we needed to see and experience the eclipse. Once the sun disappeared, so would our little pinhole of light. This is how you watched an eclipse back in 1963, through the tiny lens of a homemade pinhole camera.

So in the days after Clarke's death, this too is how I began my contest of survival. Each hour became pinpoints of light on which to focus. I couldn't look at the entire sun or the entire impact of Clarke's death at first; I had to take it one pinpoint at a time. Focus on that pinpoint of light long enough to get to the next hour and then the next. I only needed to see just beyond this thought to accomplish this.

There was no denying the truth of my circumstance. My son was killed suddenly in an automobile accident, my only child. Absorbing the reality of this could only happen in measured doses. My shock armor would not allow me to see beyond the next hour in its defensive purpose, saving my life. I was certain of my first pinpoint, my first mindset in dealing with this tragedy; I could not allow the moment of Clarke's death to become my focus. Not when the moments of his life were so incredibly rich and many. Not when his memory couldn't help but cause a smile. At the time, I couldn't know that thinking this way would be the beginning steps of my recovery from the trauma.

Chapter 48

Over the next few months following Clarke's death, I felt compelled to endure special occasions and events that quite naturally magnified his absence even more. After the funeral and the Citadel memorial service, there was Parents' Weekend. Then in November, Thanksgiving, Clarke's favorite holiday and yet, what could I be thankful for? *Thanksgiving without my son?* At various family and social drop-ins, I would have given anything to be the one serving a hot casserole and warm condolences, giving comfort rather than receiving it. Instead, when my doorbell rang, sympathy was delivered in heaping portions.

Having barely made it through Thanksgiving, Scott and I decided to be out of town for the "Big One." I just couldn't bear to be at home during Christmas, much less unwrap the tree ornaments Clarke had been making for me since he was three years old. So on Christmas morning, I awoke in Las Vegas—the one place to me that is the least like Christmas—looked out the hotel window, and began to cry. Scott held me. It just wasn't real to me. *A Christmas without Clarke?* We called family members and wished for them what we couldn't have. Next, New Year's and then Clarke's birthday—all painfully were waiting for me when we returned home from Vegas. I felt like a boxer in six consecutive fights. Bruised, bleeding, and brain dead. It was such an unbalanced and weighted conglomeration of emotional events all at once.

With Clarke's death still so recent, there hadn't been a suitable amount of time to even begin to adjust to a life without him—*there will never be enough time*—let alone to a season typically filled with rejoicing. The day after New Year's, Clarke's friends, home for the holidays, began calling. They were testing the waters with me. "Um, some of the guys and I were wondering if it might be all right to come by and see you on Clarke's birthday?" "Well, I guess it would be all right," I said, a little hoarsely at first, then finding my voice and stating my acceptance more clearly. Of course—Clarke's birthday. That would be the perfect day to see all of his friends. Acknowledging his birthday suddenly felt so right. The day he was born I felt such a happy thankfulness for the gift of my son. Clarke was born on his due date, January 6. In the Bible, it is known as the Day of Epiphany. In my life, it is the day I became a mother. It was the day that everything changed.

I knew they would come in a pack—safety in numbers—partly because they were unsure how I would react to them, partly because they were unsure how they would react to me and how their emotions would hold up being back in their familiar gathering spot. We were all hurting so much and of course still stunned that Clarke was gone from us. I called Holly and my sister Terri, asking if they might come and help me with lunch for the boys' visit. They would love to.

Chapter 49

As it was with the accident, the cell phone chain of one kid calling another, so it happened with Clarke's birthday three months after his death. Before we knew it, it had grown from his closest friends stopping by for a bite and a visit to a full-blown celebration of Clarke's life. Fifty kids, my pastors, and a few close friends showed up. Any adult who walked into this birthday party, saw the revelry and heard the laughter, immediately circled back outside just to have a private moment to take it all in. It felt to me like Clarke was in the house, his spirit bouncing off of the walls. *And if he had come clomping down the stairs in the middle of this celebration?* It would have felt so natural, I am certain we all would have looked up and said, "Yo, Clarke, where ya' been?"

It's as though I can hear Clarke saying to me, *"Yeah, this sucks way beyond anything I can think of, but what are you saying, Mom? Weren't you thrilled that I was your son? I was with you for almost twenty years—healthy, fun, loving. Your angel."*

"It wasn't long enough," I sob. "It wasn't long enough. It's *your* birthday—*you* are supposed to be *here*."

"Come on, Mom, let's you and I agree to agree; we were very blessed. I mean, look at the love we have for each other, the love that is pouring out to us … Jeez Louise. You know that I'll be with you always … listen for me, look for me, feel me. I am here with you."

"But not physically," I say. "You'll never sit on the couch with me and watch TV, just you and me holding hands. You'll never pick me up over your head to show off your muscles. You'll never extend your beautiful arms from underneath your bedcovers, eyes still closed, and simply say 'hug' ever again. You are gone, and I can't bear the weight of this truth."

"Yes, you can, Mom. You taught me how to be strong. You are strong for my friends. Remember when we looked at your high school yearbooks and you told me that story about when you were growing up, about your friends who had lost friends and it really messed them up? Promise me you won't let these friends of mine get messed up, Mom. Talk about me and remember the great times."

"I'll try."

"And promise me that you will laugh and cut the fool like you always did."

"I don't know if I can do that."

"Yes, you can ... you can do anything if you set your mind to it. Just give it some time."

"There's not enough time in the universe, son! Can't you see? I'm not that strong person you thought I was. I am so weak ... without you my life is empty! You are my life."

"Good try, Mom ... not buying it. You gave me life and love for a lifetime ... strong love, strong life. We just didn't know how long this lifetime would be, but we'll always be together, and I really need you to get this message out for me ... please, will you?"

Stubbornly, I don't answer because I know that tomorrow the same conversation will play out over and over. How long can I hold out? God knows it's taking everything I've got just to make it through this birthday gathering.

No matter how strong our collective memories and longing to see him, we knew that we must live satisfied with the memories. To this day, when all of Clarke's friends are with me, it's almost as if we are compelled to be together so that we can receive comfort and strength from each other. Standing in my kitchen, I was grateful for the fire I saw in

Clarke's friends, for that part of him I knew they would keep. It continues to be their sincere passion to carry a part of his spirit and personality into their future. As a matter of fact, on his last night alive, he had made this pointed request of his two buddies who had driven to Charleston to have dinner with him. "Let's not lose touch with each other ... really; I've been worried about us going our separate ways, you know, to different colleges and maybe jobs in different states. Let's go on keeping our friendship strong." They all agreed. Deal. The next morning he died.

Pastor Tandy said that as we continue to celebrate Clarke's life, we will continue to snub the nose on the face of death. I will always celebrate the life of my son, and by doing so, I stay in touch with the ones I love. And the one I love.

Chapter 50

The first really significant part of my shock armor fell away 126 days after Clarke died. It was the onset of winter. Until then I thought that I had fully started on my path of despair, entering by way of a tunnel named "trauma." When this first protective chunk fell away, it noticeably compromised my defenses. Grief—just waiting for this opportunity to make its malignant persona known—was now allowed to come whistling through a hole in my protective glass jar and search for a permanent resting place.

Like a demon let loose from Pandora's Box, it entered through the jar armor's first gaping, ragged hole. Grief wound around my joints and caused me to ache and shiver uncontrollably. Its full-blown *manifestation* became a physical and emotional *infestation*. Unable to control this demon, the only thing I could do on that 126th day was cry. I couldn't speak. I couldn't form a thought. I was overtaken by an acute sense of dread, abandonment, and woe. My outlook was so forlorn I knew if my grief continued like this for any length of time, that I, as a living, breathing human being, could not. At that time my mind felt like I was a hundred—or just one. I wasn't quite sure although I knew it to be the most helpless and hopeless feeling I had ever known. My vulnerability and this first awareness of grief's tireless ferocity was the closest I would come to wanting to take my life. And the worst of it had just begun.

You could say that grief is actually an entity unto itself—a force that affects every part of you. I actually have come to think of grief as a separate personality—apathetic, depressed, moody, and fearful. Grief is defined as the psychological, behavioral, social, and physical reaction to the loss of someone closely tied to an individual's identity. It also involves cognitive, emotional, spiritual, and somatic symptoms. *Can you ever be ready for something this powerful? I suppose I was as ready as I'd ever be.*

Chapter 51

"It's the code for depression," she said a little too matter-of-factly for me. After one of my therapist sessions, I had noticed a numerical code on the medical paper I was given for checkout. After a couple more appointments and the same notations on my paperwork, I asked Teresa, "What does this number mean?"

"I don't agree with that code."

"Why?" she asked.

"Well, I think that depression and sadness are two different things. I don't think that I am depressed, but I am definitely sad."

"What's the difference Stephanie?"

I thought for a moment and then said, "In my opinion, depression is a state of mind in which you can't see the end. Sadness is an emotion that moves with you. I think depression might be permanent, and sadness is temporary—it won't be with you forever. There can be an end to it; at least that's how I think about it. There's a difference."

"Okay," she said, "I'll accept that explanation. But I do want you to know, Stephanie, that you have experienced trauma in the true sense of the word. Not just sorrow or depression, but full-blown trauma." Then she said, "I am also treating you for PTSD ... Posttraumatic stress disorder—by definition a sudden event, usually involving loss of life. Like a soldier gone to battle who sees death and unthinkable horror—only to relive it over and over to the point of disorder and disruption of life." Like my circumstance—one moment I am fine, and the next I am blindsided and my world explodes all over again.

My child is dead. I still relive the accident to this day, most of the time when I least expect it, and my life has definitely been disrupted. According to Teresa, one can deal with trauma in two ways. One—recover, or two—become a victim, as in consume or be consumed, eat or be eaten. To live as a victim for the rest of your natural life is to choose and give power to death. To choose recovery is to give power to life. I chose recovery. But first, I had to accept the truth.

Chapter 52

You can do this, Stephanie. Remember: One pinhole, one reveal, and one hour at a time. Once I decided I could live, I knew that this commitment for me meant all or nothing. I wanted to live in honor of the relationship that Clarke and I shared. My first step was to admit and acknowledge the truth. But how could I possibly face it head on?

The challenge of facing the truth reminded me of when I was a kid, hell, an adult, too, for that matter. During a scary movie, I still hold my hand in front of my eyes. Then I separate my fingers, one by one, taking the fright in a little at a time, knowing that to see the whole thing at once would just be too much. Yet when my hand is totally removed, what I imagined to be so scary isn't nearly as frightful as I thought. While all this seemed like taking baby steps, what I was really accomplishing was a giant leap of faith, feeling my way slowly while adapting to an unfamiliar new life—a life without Clarke. I constantly reminded myself that I was here *first—before* grief moved in. Life can be gone in an instant, a breath, a heartbeat, yet we all live as if we will live forever. We walk around, shop, work out, go to sports events, schedule, plan, run here and there, caught up in what we are supposed to do instead how we are supposed to be. Years ago, a counselor said to me, "we all need to be more 'humans being' than 'humans doing.'" I've never forgotten that.

Chapter 53

Even now, there are times that I still ask myself, "This didn't really happen, did it? Is Clarke really gone forever?" With every part of who I am, I wish not to believe it. But my questions are futile. Futile because the answers will always be the same and the whys will never be understood. I learned quickly that questions with no answers come with a high price. The "what ifs" of death are a form of bargaining. Each question connects with another, and before you're even aware of it, you are trapped in a victim mindset maze, frozen in the inability to reconnect with the world around you. The hours that I have spent wishing, hoping, and praying that this didn't really happen have eaten away countless weeks of my life. And those famous seven stages of grief—shock, denial, anger, depression, bargaining, pain, and acceptance? They really are an arduous spiral, constantly going in one direction and then another. Grief is not linear. You don't get a diploma for going through one phase or graduating to the next stage of grief. More times than I care to remember, I found myself in the middle of this funnel cloud, assaulted at every turn, and just when I thought I could catch my breath, I'd get slammed in the head or the heart by grief's debris. *Debris—that's how I think of the seven stages of grief.*

It is so very difficult to accept the "unnatural order" of a child dying before a parent. Even though as a "human doing" I demanded the answers—as a "human being" I needed to be still, reflect, and honor the life of my beloved Clarke. Slowly, eventually the truth did start to set me free; at least admitting it did. It was my first baby step—a pinhole peek at trying to live a life without my son.

I like to think I am here and Clarke is there. Where is there? I don't know for certain. I just know it isn't here. But one thing I do know for certain; one day I'll be there, too.

Chapter 54

Of all my truthful admissions, this is the hardest: the only unconditional love that exists in this world is from a parent to a child. The importance of this would absolutely reveal itself to you if your only child died. Having thought about it after Clarke left me, I recalled this unconditional love that flowed endlessly from my great grandmother to her sons, from my grandmother to my mother, from my mother to her children, and from me to Clarke. As if the miracle of birthing a child comes with this most precious gift of all—love without conditions. No matter what the child could do or would do or does do or did do, there is nothing—nothing—that wavers this unconditional acceptance that comes from inside the protective womb to that child to whom you give life.

I marvel and deeply understand those mothers who visit their children on death row, knowing that their child has committed the most heinous crime imaginable, but still they continue to love them. Hurt, defeated—maybe, emotionally crushed, but still they bestow love. I saw it with me and my four siblings. No matter how many times the phone would ring with the latest violations, my mother would defend us with her last breath.

I think about my husband Scott and how helpless he must feel—knowing that the very best he can give me will never be enough to take me to my very best place again. Even when he shovels in every bit of love he can possibly feel and muster and show, it will never fill the hole created by Clarke's death. I feel for him. I love him almost as much as I love Clarke, but I know that my love for him as a husband and his love for me as a wife will never be a love without conditions.

For parents who are fortunate to have more children, you still have this unconditional love. For me, it died with Clarke, and sadly, slowly, I realized that there is no one left on earth who I would ever love in the same way I loved my son. This finality of unconditional love lost still sneaks into my memories. To this day and for eternity, the loss of being able to love unconditionally will be my greatest and deepest hollow space.

Chapter 55

Like a freight train out of nowhere, leaving our outer shells intact but our insides mangled and forever changed. Only when I began grief therapy did I actually come to understand the truth behind Scott's analogy of the effect Clarke's death would have in our lives.

Upon the impact of the news, the experiences, emotions, feelings, and personality that comprised the real Miss Stephanie—my entire being—bolted for the hills. I abandoned myself. As I came to realize much later, those parts of me had simply gone on sabbatical, waiting to regain strength and return again, only when the shock soldiers had completed their duty. Shock had to have its space, and my essence had to make room for it: it was these shock soldiers that were keeping me alive—insuring I performed the most basic of human functions. Bathe, nourish, eliminate, walk, and cry— all accomplished by the autopilots now housed in my body. It felt like "tabula rasa"—a blank slate—a baby who had no impressions with which to judge life. It was more than I could handle, so for a while, I was content to let the soldiers do what they did best—protect me from the despair of it all.

I knew, eventually, the old me would undergo the transformation to a new me, filling again with emotions and feelings as my insides worked to right themselves. All of my spaces, once overflowing with the me from *before* the accident, were now hollow spaces waiting to be infused with a different set of instincts, a new code of living, a new standard for happiness, and the knowledge that, from here on in, every day would be a struggle.

I recently watched a video of me taken six months before the accident that took my baby—my face is beaming, my laughter true, and my eyes clear and alive. When I look at photos of me since Clarke was killed, it's as if part of my essence has been diluted like too many copies on a low ink cartridge. I am diminished from within—an instamatic snapshot in my photo album since 1975, colors turned to acid orange and yellow covered with a milky haze.

Eventually and tentatively, my new instincts and impressions found their way to the hollow spaces and rested there a while. There, they would grow and expand. Holly and I actually gave this expansion period a name—the pause button—because when you are experiencing the death of your child, you are barraged with a shower of emotions and feelings. If you act upon every one, you would become angry, impulsive, foolish, and dangerous. So I learned to feel the first tinge of a feeling's intent, and then allowed it to nestle into its hollow space first, before determining if it should become a new feeling. A new part of Stephanie, or just another passing knee jerk impulse? The pause button taught me some very important lessons, like—it's okay to say, "I don't know" or "I'm not sure." It's okay to be uncertain of how we feel at every given moment; God forbid we should be unable to answer every question asked of us. "I'll get back to you," "I don't know how I feel about that right now," "Let me think about it, okay?" Let me tell you—it's all okay!

Chapter 56

Say there, would you be looking for your old pal Stephanie—the me before Clarke died? Impossible. You might as well ask a stone to bring forth water. I knew that September 10, 2005, had changed everything, 100%. Stem to stern. Tear duct to brain cells. I knew I would never be the same again, especially to those who knew me best. The outside was still familiar except for the fire in my eyes and the gut laugh that used to escape so easily. Sure, I appeared normal on the outside, but my inside was anything but. Strange, but if you look and somewhat act like the same person you were before an emotional tragedy, humans just can't comprehend your pain. Their brains immediately register "normal." My husband said that because I seemed the same on the outside, it was easy for people to become "lulled" into believing that I was my old normal self. Ever so easily, your friends fall back into thinking things are back the way they used to be. *Still thinking I'm the strong one.* Still expecting that I should be sensitive to their needs when I truly needed to be sensitive to my own. This is a tough one; quite honestly, I had used up the majority of my sympathy, empathy, and every other "pathy" you can think of on me. Myself. I. If the people in my life can't understand this, I am truly sorry.

I have agonized over this segment of retelling my experience and this particular chapter for many months. How can I say what I need to say without pissing people off? How can I try to explain the mindset of a parent who endures the death of a child? How does one's interaction with family and friends change when something like this happens? No one can know how this feels unless you are a parent who has lost a child—the true unnatural order. Yes, losing anyone close to you in the natural order of life is sad, but it most definitely is not tragic. Losing your child is tragic, and for some it is a tragedy from which they never recover.

All I can do is to tell you what I think and the process that I used to survive. It's especially painful, *as if the pain can be metered*, when your only child dies. There are no other children on which to bestow your unconditional love and share their future. With an only child, your hopes of becoming a grandparent are gone. Having a son or daughter-in-law, gone. Neither will ever happen. An additional layer of pain, according to grief experts, is when your child dies between the ages of seventeen and twenty—*just shove another knife in my gut*. I thought those who knew me best would instinctively get this—for God's sake!—but sadly they didn't, and some still don't. It's not that I can't share happy news (a few endearing comments or gripes is fine) but I just feel it absolutely rude—perhaps even ignorantly cruel to go on and on about subjects like grandchildren; *don't you realize I'll never have one?* Or bitching about your son or daughter who's the same age as Clarke was when he died or would be now if alive? *If only I had Clarke here to bitch about.* I am not, nor will I accept being the person on the listening end of these discussions!

The journey ends with me—childless. Someone so graciously said in response to this very observation I had voiced, "Steph, having one child was your choice." Thanks. If I had spent my life as a more delicate or passive person, maybe people would have been more mindful of the things they said to me. But I have always been a strong, forthright person able to take most any comment on the chin. Unfortunately, and quite remarkably, after the accident, few chose to modify their approach to me, which I found incredibly insensitive. I also found myself becoming increasingly impatient with pettiness—with overuse of words and phrases like "disaster," "tragic," and "the worst thing that could happen." With grief there is always anger, but whenever *my* anger dared to rear its head, many people took offense and, in turn, became defensive. Instead of allowing me to vent, they took it personally. There were even those who expressed a desire for me to grieve deeply, fall on my knees, and weep with them. Why? *Partly to share my sadness and partly because they wanted to satisfy* ***their*** *need to grieve with* ***me.*** At these times, it wasn't about me at all. It was about them. And visits to the cemetery? Am I to be judged because I can't bear going there? Occasionally I go by to collect the weathered mementos and faded love notes, but I don't linger long. Clarke is not there! He is with me. I now know that grief is as individual as a fingerprint or a snowflake—each one's experience different from another. This is *my* experience.

My most important life-after-death lesson became my personal credo. *I will honor my feelings.* New. Old. All mingled together. What you see and what you get is the new Stephanie. Like it or lump it—my life will never be the same. And *I* will never be the same. I will grieve for Clarke forever. And I will *never* get over it. But will I and can I and do I choose to still live a life that's good? Absolutely. To this day, I continue to honor these feelings and explain as best I can. "Sorry, I don't have it to give you right now." Maybe not ever.

Chapter 57

Several people asked if I had started my Thank You notes. Are you kidding me? It's not just a thank you note—it's my heart breaking all over again every time I even thought about writing one. Like when I wrote Clarke's obituary, unable to get through the first word. So I decided, rather than put myself through the torture, I would create just one Thank You message and have it printed on cards. If I wanted to include a personal note, I could. Otherwise the card would universally express what I wanted to say to everyone. To this day, people tell me that this card is still on their refrigerator, or in their Bible; they read it during holidays and are instantly reminded to be thankful for their lives and the lives of their children. I never guessed that something that had helped me get through this "etiquette acknowledgment" would help others, as well. Maybe one of those moments when I honored *my* feelings first, rather than doing what I thought others expected of me—well, let's just say it quite possibly encouraged others to honor their own feelings, too. Maybe for the first time. I knew Clarke would approve.

Clarke Gibért Russell

January 6, 1986   September 10, 2005

~ Show Faith ~ Eat and Eat Well ~ Start a Trend ~ Smile ~

~ Root for the Underdog ~ Appreciate Beauty ~ Make Lifelong Friends ~ Ask Questions ~

How do we begin to express our gratitude for what we have received these past weeks? We feel, as you did, when we learned the shocking news our precious Clarke was gone, that words are inadequate. What can we say? What can we do? Just as you, our family and friends, we have been overcome with sorrow and lost in grief. Still, you came to comfort us in our grief. You came with raw hearts and tears, hugs of comfort, shared fears, helping hands, food to eat and a host of prayer. Your love held us up when we were too weak to stand. Your prayers bolstered our Faith in God and He gave us strength to face another day. For this, we are forever humbled and thankful.

Clarke Gibért Russell was a wonderful son and we are so very proud of, and thankful for his life, his accomplishments, his legacy and his spirit. We have experienced peace through an honest and loving relationship with him, happiness through his ability to live each day and make us laugh, and respect through his determination to achieve his personal best. Through Clarke's life, our lives will forever be changed.

Clarke lived 7,192 days on earth, and in an instant he was called to his Heavenly Father. We will, and pray that you will, celebrate the days we were allowed to spend with him.

From our hearts, thank you

~ Work Out ~ Learn ~ LOVE Unconditionally ~ LIVE Fearlessly ~ Climb a Mountain ~

~ Be True ~ Dance ~ Laugh ~ Fish ~ "Chill" ~ Sing ~ Sleep ~

Eight things that I, or anyone grieving a death, does not wish to hear.

It was God's plan.
Phooey and double phooey. God does not plan to cause pain and suffering. His plan is not to take a wonderful child and friend and cause anyone the depths of this kind of sorrow.
So very strange ... how a knowingly loving and compassionate God gets the blame, or the "credit" for an untimely death. It's just not so.

God needed him or her more than you did.
This is simply not possible. Period. End of conversation.

Just think, he or she will never have to feel pain again.
What exactly does this mean anyway? Life is about options, to feel or not to feel. Death takes that away.

Everything happens for a reason.
Nothing happens for a reason. Things happen from making choices. Death is random. There are no reasons, only possible explanations.

It was his or her time.
No it wasn't. It's never time for a young, vibrant and innocent man to die in a violent automobile accident. Call it untimely—just don't call it "his time." That's bull.

He or she is in a better place.
Unless Clarke is in the Keys, fishing, I don't think so.

Just give it time.
There's not enough time.

Nothing at all
As much as the above statements (each truly expressed several times to me) didn't make sense, making no statements is inexcusable. *"I'm so sorry"* is truly enough. For those who simply "don't know what to say", buy a card that says it for you. To not say or do anything is far worse and more offensive than saying the wrong thing. *What—you don't think Clarke or I deserve a word or deed of acknowledgment or sympathy?* You can't leave *your* comfort zone long enough to recognize that I'll never have a comfort zone again, ever. *You're uncomfortable?* Pathetic.

Chapter 58

And so, ever so slowly, I've come to know that grief will live with me forever. It will always be in the shadows, always waiting to emerge. Sometimes I know when grief will appear: anniversaries, birthdays, college graduations, weddings, and holidays. Other times it comes out of nowhere and overshadows who I am. Without warning—a smell, a song, a commercial featuring a little boy making treats in the kitchen with his mom who looks remarkably like Clarke at that age— grief will overtake me. These are the hardest times because they are the most everyday, normal circumstances. Grief is so oppressive—like a huge boulder that I want to move so I can breathe, it sits heavy on my personal ground. You see, when Clarke died, my future with him died, too.

So before grief eclipsed me and who I was, I chose to embrace and dance with the grief. I knew if I tried to ignore it, it would always come back stronger than twenty mules with a vengeance and a kick in the ass. By embracing this powerful force, I am positive that I have lessened its impact on my life. Try it sometime, with anything that bothers you, from the tragic to the petty. Instead of using your energy to oppose it which is *defensive*, embrace it, and amazingly you will find that its power and negativity diminish. And you, in turn, become more accepting and stronger.

Bottom line is this: I have learned to coexist with grief; we will grow old together—my grief and I—spinning 'round and 'round on this dance floor called life. For certain, I'm committed to taking the lead with authority, strength, and the knowledge that there will always be just one more dance.

Chapter 59

None of us are immortal. The one truth we know immediately, as soon as we can possibly know anything, is that some day we will die. It is an irrefutable fact that we are the most sure of and, at the same time, the most unsure of. Every hour and day that we live, we are one breath closer to the moment that our flesh will cease to exist. But that flesh and two legs simply give posture to who we are on the inside. This is my new perspective: While all of us will physically wither and decompose, the spirit that God has breathed into this receptacle of flesh is what matters the very most. Each of us is to take heart, finding courage and comfort in celebrating life well lived. What we have done. Who we have helped. Who we have made laugh, or have lifted with a kind word. What we have learned and shared with others. I think what angers me the most is that death takes away all of one's options. *What color shirt to wear. What menu item to order. What to be when you grow up. Do you want to grow up?* With that being said, I will share what this thought has revealed to me, the one notion that gives me a certain hope and inspiration.

We are only human. When someone dies, we miss the flesh because we want and miss that which we can touch, hug, kiss, stroke, see. In turn, that which we cannot see or touch, we do not understand because we do not want to understand. The fact is, we are afraid of death—what we know of it and *what we do not know*. Where do our essence (**who** we are instead of **what**) and our spirit go? Where do they soar? Who can tell us? Neither the living nor the dead.

Here, in the South, when someone asks, "How ya' doin'?" I always say, "I'm all right in the shade if the tree don't fall."

Did my tree fall? Yes. Can I sit quietly beneath the shade of a different tree and feel the whisper of Clarke's spirit on my cheek? Yes. Will I continue to try to be the person that my son loved? Yes, who Clarke was is now a part of who I am. While I never imagined that I would ever have the capacity to hold on to this much faith, I am not afraid.

For me, this tragedy remains beyond understanding. I finally admit there is no answer to "Why?" And while an accident may have taken away Clarke's flesh, my son will not have truly died unless I let him.

When I look at the difference his nineteen years made in our world, it is with intense necessity I believe that what matters most is that he is still with me, beside me, above me, and in me. Each breath I take, I feel his sweet breath with mine; his heartbeat, just a fraction of a second offbeat.

Am I sad? It is a sadness beyond feeling. Missing Clarke is an irreversible ache in my heart. It is *a pain that I bear for the crown that I wear.* I wear my crown proudly because for a while I was the First Queen Mother, my Clarke, the Prince Son. No one will ever take that away from me.

For me, it's impossible to own the memories without having the pain. And so I have made my choice. To release Clarke's memory simply because it is too painful would literally diminish me as a person, and diminish Clarke's existence in my life. So, yes, I will grieve, but in doing so will remain as close to Clarke as I can. And as close to being "me" again as possible. I choose to conjure up finite memories constantly, with laughter, with love, and with tears. He was and continues to be my angel—an angel that I dress with every morning—

putting on my memories of Clarke like my favorite tattered jeans and oversized Abercrombie oxford shirt, warm from the dryer, soft, and comfortable. I honor how this makes me feel. If I want to cry, I cry. I smile. I laugh and share a memory with my husband or with anybody. I nestle in it, sleep in it, and wrap it around me. It's how I'm keeping Clarke.

"If you are grieving a death, I encourage you to do something—anything—in that person's honor. Plant a tree, hang a picture, create a new tradition or repeat cherished ones. Play their music, read their words, smile at the thought of them. Talk about them. Remember that love never dies and who they were will forever be a part of who we are."

Keep on Keeping. Stephanie

The oldest of five children, the author grew up in Columbia, South Carolina. Currently, she and her husband Scott live in the Upstate of South Carolina. They are keeping Clarke through a food ministry—Clarke's Kitchen—at Eastminister Presbyterian Church in Simpsonville, a perpetual scholarship in Clarke's memory at the Citadel in Charleston...and planting trees...